WHAT  TO QUALIFY

Nursing Through a Pandemic

By

Sarah Hepworth-Dodds

Copyright © Sarah Hepworth-Dodds 2022
This book is sold subject to the condition that it shall not, by way of trade or otherwise, be lent, resold, hired out, or otherwise circulated without the publisher's prior consent in any form of binding or cover other than that in which it is published and without a similar condition including this condition being imposed on the subsequent publisher.
The moral right of Sarah Hepworth-Dodds has been asserted.
ISBN: 9798429133935

While all the stories in this book are true, some names and identifying details have been changed to protect the privacy of the people involved.

This book is dedicated to a nation that suffered at the hand of a pandemic. For those we lost, for those we saved, and for those whose lives were changed.

CONTENTS

ACKNOWLEDGEMENTS i
INTRODUCTION 1
CHAPTER 1 *The Blues* 3
CHAPTER 2 *The Unexpected* 17
CHAPTER 3 *Is This The Start?* 28
CHAPTER 4 *And So, It Begins* 40
CHAPTER 5 *We Laugh and We Cry* 51
CHAPTER 6 *It's Nothing Personal* 64
CHAPTER 7 *Times Are Changing* 72
CHAPTER 8 *Good News Stories* 82
CHAPTER 9 *New Year, New You* 92
CHAPTER 10 *Mother Nature* 109
CHAPTER 11 *Are We Turning A Corner?* 120
CHAPTER 12 *We All Have Our Weaknesses* 137
CHAPTER 13 *Times, They Are A Changing* 149
CHAPTER 14 *You Couldn't Write It* 160
CHAPTER 15 *Time For A Change* 171
CHAPTER 16 *Final Thoughts* 188
ABOUT THE AUTHOR 190

ACKNOWLEDGEMENTS

Being able to 'tell a good story' is a lot easier than writing a good story, one of which would not have been possible if it weren't for the unconditional support and encouragement of my amazing husband Steven, beautiful children Emily and Mark, and my parents Lesley and Chris. Without you all by my side, none of this would have been possible. Thank you.

The main heroes in this story are the NHS healthcare professionals who, throughout the pandemic, have worked endlessly to keep the nation safe, embracing unprecedented times and making every contact count.

@TheGeordieNurse
www.Thegeordienurse.com

INTRODUCTION

This is me, a mature student who took the plunge and started training as an Adult Nurse at the tender age of 37, and what a time to do it – being the class of 2020 was one of the most challenging times for student nurses and an experience in itself.

In 2017 the Department of Health and Education decided to remove the bursary for all nursing students. Now the only option is self-funding through the loan process of Student Finance England, accruing an average of £40,000 debt once qualified and 3,500 hours unpaid work in various clinical roles. It was not a choice for the uncommitted. It had been a childhood dream to become a nurse, the training and experiences I had were second to none, but nothing could prepare me for what was yet to come. When I embarked on this journey, little did I know I would relocate to the nation's capital amidst a world-changing pandemic.

This book is the journey of my first nine months as a newly qualified nurse, the highs and lows, the expected and the unexpected, the tears and laughter, and the bonds created through tragedy and success. These are written in retrospect of my experiences, a true account of my own journey, feelings, and opinions. They do not reflect the NHS and their efforts; they endured to preserve the life of the nation through this challenging time. This fight was not mine alone, I was part of an amazing team, much like the teams throughout the world all fighting for one cause, a team of heroes.

Due to the sensitive nature, anonymity will be enforced by the complete use of alternate names and places for all mentioned, with the exclusion of myself.

The inspiration for this book is my amazing husband and children who, throughout the whole experience, were there for me, my own little cheerleading squad listening and encouraging me through every step, my reason for carrying on, for that I am forever in their debt.

CHAPTER 1

THE BLUES

It was my final year as a student and my son has secured a once-in-a-lifetime opportunity to study and play American Football in London. My studies meant I was unable to join him and my husband in London, so my daughter took a year out from starting university and stayed in Newcastle with me. Living apart was hard, travelling after 13-hour shifts between the two was exhausting and emotionally draining but we are a committed family and were making the most of it.

In February 2020, I had my first interview for a nursing position in London, on my birthday of all days! I had smashed it, securing my dream job as a staff nurse in urgent care. Things were looking up and there was light at the end of a long, hard three years, we celebrated and looked to the future.

It had been less than four weeks since my interview when the unthinkable happened. The world was hit with a devastating pandemic, a pandemic that would change the lives of millions forever, mine included.

It was mid-March and mid-week, I had headed straight to London after finishing a three-day stretch of 13-hour shifts on placement, I had packed my son and his belongings up and we had headed back to Newcastle, fearing that things would only get worse, my husband had followed the next day.

It was less than 72 hours later when it was announced 'lockdown' had been initiated in the United Kingdom. At this point I was thankful that I had all my family in one place, and they were safe, but the world was in a whole lot of pain, a pain that would become very real to us as a family in the months ahead.

University had been changed to online, final year management placements were looking unlikely. It was the end of April and the Government, in agreement with the Nursing and Midwifery Council, decided that all nurses in their final year were to be deployed on the frontline to relieve some of the pressures of qualified staff. Twelve weeks was all I had needed to qualify, my final twelve weeks were tough, but we were finally getting paid, the new role of an aspirant nurse had been created and those willing would have now been deployed at the forefront of healthcare.

I had been one of the lucky ones, I had avoided a Covid positive ward and been deployed to a neurology ward. As challenging as the patients were, I had been a vital part of an amazing supportive team who guided me through some tough times, times that would carry me through the next nine months.

It was the end of August 2020 and I had just completed my 12-week management placement; the final scores were in, and I had qualified as an adult nurse, three long years of studying and 3,500 hours of unpaid placements and I had finally done it, Nurse Sarah at your service. However, damn Covid meant I was a few weeks later in finishing than anticipated, therefore had less than a week to pack up my home in Newcastle-Upon-Tyne and move to London. To add more insult, we were denied the opportunity to have a graduation ceremony or ball, how my family would have loved to have seen me graduate with the gown and mortarboard hat, however it was not to be, and I had a job to do, there were more important things to worry about.

A week later I had moved from my hometown of Newcastle to the nation's capital, and the email had arrived, I had my PIN (a registration number needed to practice), it's official, I was a registered nurse, well once I had paid my £120 registration fee. Yep, that's right 120 smackers each year, seventeen bottles of wine or twenty treble vodkas and coke, what a privilege! But it's a requirement of holding my Nursing licence, a badge of honour so to speak.

I was currently 267 miles away from friends and family, ready to start my nursing career in the UK's capital. The phrase 'All the gear and nee idea' felt very apt, a phrase I had become very accustomed to over the past 18 months. For example, when you're standing in a supermarket with your mask on and the idiots in front of you have masks, visors, gloves, and full-blown theatre gowns on just to do their shop. They then reach over you now with their visor sitting on their forehead, their mask under their chin, asking is there any better dates at the back.

"What the actual fuck?" I had responded with, the looks on their faces were as though I had threatened to kill them … 'all the gear and nee idea' at its finest. I believe I am quite a tolerant person, but have little to no patience, definitely not suffering fools lightly, which is now why I do most of my shopping online.

It was finally my first day as a nurse in the big smoke and I had my own little cheerleading squad waiting for me at the bottom of the stairs, my husband beaming with pride and excitement and my adult children, two zombies who had obviously been dragged from their beds to wish me luck as I had left. Looking back these three humans were the reason I survived the next nine months. Everything I did, I did to keep them safe and make them proud.

Until this point, I hadn't been nervous at all but the fear of letting them down had suddenly hit me and I could feel the nervous poo making its way through my body, that sickly feeling that at any moment a little tortoise was about to pop its head out … oh my what a day this was going to be. Little squeeze of the cheeks, brave smile on my face, and off I trotted.

As I had begun the walk down the bank towards the hospital, everything I had thought I knew about nursing, the human body, medications, had all gone, poof, just like that I had an empty brain. I couldn't even remember the name of my unit or my managers. I had ruffled frantically in my pocket trying to find my phone with any details that would have helped, but before I knew it, I was at the door. Everyone was rushing past to start their shifts on time and there was me like a bumbling idiot, a fish out of water, barely knowing my own name, my nerves had got the better of me and I was bricking it.

A deep, stern voice had emanated from the big guy on the left.

"Can we help you?" and in the blink of an eye the nerves had vanished, and the fear had set in, two burley men dressed for war in security gear stood over me, a far cry away from the makeshift porter security in Newcastle. With no ID badge, profusely sweating and obviously squeezing my cheeks whilst sounding like an extra from *Geordie Shore*, I tried to explain how it was my first day and I had no idea where I was supposed to be or who I was supposed to meet. Needless to say, they weren't impressed, but waited patiently as I found the details of my unit and manager. You would like to think they would have just let me be on my merry way, nope, they escorted me personally to where I needed to be, all the way you could have heard a pin drop. Literally so embarrassing, I had rocked up on the ward, on my first day, with my own disgruntled entourage.

*

I had been waiting three years for my 'blues', however today was not the day; my uniform hadn't arrived, and I was guided to the changing room where scrubs awaited me. They were several washed-out shades of blue, but nevertheless blue, unlike my previous experience of scrubs where the option was salmon pink, very washed-out salmon pink.

Scrubs were great, they were loose fitting, you didn't have to wash them, and wearing them was like working in your pyjamas.

As good as they sounded, I had previously had a very unpleasant experience wearing scrubs ...

It had all started in my second year of training, seven weeks in theatres and from day one there was a notable frequency of flatulence, basically I had farted my way through the entire placement, a most unpleasant experience. I had constantly questioned whether it had been something I had eaten. Or was it the newfound freedom my stomach was experiencing with the elasticated waist of the scrubs? I have no idea still to this day, but seven weeks in scrubs severely breaking wind led to an unprecedented personal demand for clean underwear and Sudocrem, I most definitely did not live the dream during that placement.

The mere thought of finding neat little corners to let it rip again, walking like a duck whilst squeezing my cheeks and praying that they didn't smell didn't appeal to me. New job, new day, new pants, surely not? Then the added dilemma of 'Did I tell my manager of my condition?' Was it a condition? How would she react when I tried to explain that I had such a problem and it was that "I just can't stop farting in scrubs"? Reading this out loud, I should have be sectioned surely. Was it too soon in the relationship to disclose such personal defects, or would she be compassionate and totally relate? Yep, all the above meant that I kept it to myself and soldiered on, praying for the best, ensuring a bland diet and plenty of clean underwear were constantly at hand.

Flatulence aside I was now a fully-fledged nurse about to receive my first handover. As I approached the nurse's station, everyone had greeted me with an unnerving amount of enthusiasm, as the day progressed it was apparent as to why. It had been crazy busy; everything was so different! Overwhelmed was an understatement – I had felt as though I was drowning. I was clueless, hopeless if I were to be honest, but I survived and that's all I could ask for, on the plus side there was very little action from the bottom, could I have been cured or was it luring me into a sense of false security? I had been cured, don't get me wrong I still had moments, even days of farting, but not to the previous extremes, it was a relief as scrubs were soon to be a permanent fixture.

*

As the weeks progressed, I adapted to the craziness. I had forgotten about pre-filled flushes and having to draw up my own became second nature, falling over equipment in the corridors became a natural hazard, having to draw up medications on any bit of clean surface I could find had somehow became the norm and I had mastered the art of negotiation with the doctor's team, I felt as though I was winning. Feeling a sense of winning was great but very rare because as nurses we were constantly fighting fires; just surviving the day with your pin intact, now that's winning, it's not what you have achieved but how you have survived that makes or breaks you.

Standard practice for newly qualified nurses is to complete a minimum two-week period of supervision. Being in a new trust I thought I would have maybe gotten more time to adjust, but the resources weren't available, so I had to bite the bullet, put on my big girl pants, and as they say in Newcastle just 'crack on with it'.

The two weeks of supervision was uneventful to say the least, it was now time for my first day on my own and I finally had my blues. I had opted for dresses mainly because as a student we could only wear tunic and trousers, a dress would be a nice change and looking back a good choice. However, I had not expected the unwanted attention wearing a dress would bring from the elderly population, nor its intensity. Not to discriminate, the female patients loved the dresses; getting back to the olden days they would often say 'Just needs a belt and a nice hat and you're good to go', but the males, they were in a different league. From dropping things on the floor, slight stroke of your waist when helping them out of the bed, to the shouting across the ward.

"Show us a bit more leg!"

To say it politely they were trying old beggars, but it was all in good spirit, no harm meant. Flattering as it was, it did become a bit repetitive throughout thirteen-hour shifts.

I must admit though, one particular young man (in his eighties), who I shall refer to as a shrunken Father Christmas, blew my mind. As with a lot of patients who suffer a urinary tract infection, they can become disorientated and delusional, three-night shifts of constant "Tuck me in, nurse", "Give me a night kiss" I can forgive, pleasantly confused as we would say. However, I had been passing his bed when a little voice said, "Nurse can you help me back to bed?"

"Of course," I had responded. "It's so good to see you getting back to yourself," I assured him but then with a little touch of my behind that sweet little old voice said, "Care to join me?" Maybe the flirting and innuendos weren't down to confusion?

As I declined the ever-thoughtful invite, he had responded with a snigger and "You won't ever get a better offer, I'm telling you, you're almost past your use-by date." Cheeky bugger! As I chuckled and tucked him into bed I had responded, "You're probably right, but I don't think my husband would be too happy." I loved a quick, witty come back of a patient and his didn't disappoint, "I won't tell if you don't" was the icing on the cake. "Have a nap before you get the both of us in trouble," I whispered back. How could I not smile, his face was beaming, eyes with a glint of happiness, he was on the mend, and it warmed my heart to see.

Until this day that line has stayed with me, and I still find myself having a chuckle, my little Father Christmas and "You won't get a better offer". It's little gems like this that makes nursing great, the moments when you feel like you had made a difference in someone's day.

*

Another day begins, it's 7.30 a.m. and the handover began as follows:

'We have a lovely lady patient whose 106 years of age, came in with Total Loss of Consciousness, declined in mobility, hoping to get home today.' My first thoughts were of a frail old lady bedbound waiting for me to wash and feed her, but this couldn't have been further from the truth. There she sat in her chair dressed for the day, not a hair out of place, a full face of makeup, legs crossed, playing on her iPad. I couldn't help but smile with admiration as there I stood, my hair seventy percent dry shampoo, the only effort made was a touch of mascara.

"Don't beat yourself up," I told myself, it was probably the night staff, even so she did look the part.

As I greeted her with a big smile, I had blurted out like fan girl, "Wow I hope you haven't gone to all that effort for me!" It was then I realised that this probably wasn't the greeting I should have gone with, she glared right at me with the biggest grimace that seemed like it lasted a lifetime before responding.

"Shame that can't be said for you." At this point in time, I remember feeling mortified, startled and for once had no comeback until she broke that grimace, "Only joking, you'll do, we can work on your makeup together later." I had politely smiled and agreed, however my mind was saying 'not a hope in hell', all that effort which, don't get me wrong, I appreciated, but up close it looked like it been applied in the dark with a paint roller.

I had begun to start preparing her medications when I had heard a mild cough, and a little voice.

"Can you do me last? I'm in the middle of a game," she said as she tapped the screen of her iPad.

"A game?" I asked.

"Yep, I'm playing poker with my friend in the states, and I am winning so come back later!"

"Very funny," I said, "now really, what are you doing?" She was playing poker with people in the States, currently £60 up and aiming for more. As I had looked over her shoulder at her profile picture I queried, "Is that you?"

"Don't be daft," she had responded, "that's my granddaughter. I don't want them thinking they are playing an old hag," she cackled, very hag-like. Hmm, she was far from an old hag, what she was, was a little dark horse; glamour, gambling, and unsparingly deceitful – I couldn't have been more in love with a patient if I tried, she had all the sass and glamour of a dynasty character.

Throughout that day she had kept me entertained with her wild stories and antics, I think she had sex in more places than I have had hot dinners, not one for the faint hearted but, to be fair, a person could no doubt do a hell of a lot in a hundred and six years.

"Did you know that getting sand in your crack makes your skin smooth?"

Well there was a vision that wouldn't be leaving my mind anytime soon, however my mouth had politely responded, "Every day is a school day." I literally had nothing else. This patient left nothing to one's imagination!

The women and men on the unit were separated, but this lady was persistent in wanting to look at the 'Totty', her persistence had weighed me down, so on her discharge we had taken a swift detour round the male bay, and surprisingly she didn't disappoint.

"Hello boys," she had shouted as I wheeled her past the beds, arm in the air as though she was the queen. Needless to say they enjoyed the view just as much as she had, it was great to see the smiles – please let me be like this at her age!

My first day going solo and she had made it the most memorable. With the most amazing outlook on life at 106 years young, she was ready for the world. I'm not sure if the world was ready for her but I was in total awe. She was a reminder to me to never judge a book by its cover.

A great first day.

*

It was a Saturday morning, my gentlemen patient was in bed laughing and joking with me about the 'Oliver Twist' breakfast, a simple choice of porridge, cereal, and bread and butter, we laughed and joked.

"At least there's a choice or white or brown bread," he quipped and we chuckled. It's quite an awful display of what's on offer and the lunches and evening meals are abysmal, all pre-ordered and if you're lucky to get what you have ordered then it's a few beeps in a microwave and popped on a plate, very rarely is there availability of fresh fruit, just a whole load of stodge.

As I had walked away to my next patient, I heard a croaking sound as though someone was choking. As I had turned and looked, he was struggling to catch his breath, rubbing his chest, pointing in distress, his face turned an awful grey colour as I rushed over.

"You okay?" I had asked and he shook his head, his eyes bulging wide, as tears strolled down his face. I swiftly leant across him and pulled the emergency buzzer, shouting for help, he was unable to speak, his eyes widen filled with the look of fear, I know it's bad, my heart sank.

"You're going to be okay," I re-assured him, "help is on its way."

The doctors rushed in, I began to handover.

Name, age ... then suddenly it hit me. He was DNAR! Do Not Attempt Resuscitation (DNAR for short), a protocol that's put in place when it is agreed that performing CPR will not be effective nor improve the quality of life if performed on an individual. As nurses, we appreciate the decisions of the doctors and patients, majority of the time we're even thankful that they are in place, but in real-life situations its heart-breaking.

My very own Oliver Twist and I felt cold and helpless. The words rattled around in my head as the realisation set in that the priority had changed from 'save his life' to 'make him comfortable.' He had such a tight grip on my hand, he must have been in so much pain. My colleagues rushed to get pain relief, it seemed like they were gone forever and, before I knew it, it was too late as I felt his grip loosen and eventually drop. I removed my gloves and held his hand to re-assure and comfort him as his eyes gently closed, he had slipped away peacefully.

My heart was wrenched, I was in shock as he had passed very quickly, one minute we were laughing and joking the next he was gone. Although this was the first time I had met this man, I still felt a deep loss, life is so precious. I looked up at the nurses standing there at the edge of the bed, speechless with their filled syringes, their shock and despair apparent beneath their masks.

"He's gone!" I had exclaimed and the look of disbelief and sadness was clearly visible in their eyes, as nurses we are there to preserve life, but some days it's like fighting a losing battle. I laid his hand down on the bed and wished him sweet dreams.

It's not in question that we hadn't done anything wrong, it just highlights the importance of how quick life can be taken away from us. Do Not Attempt Resuscitation orders are not placed lightly on patients; there are several factors to take into consideration – damage potentially caused by doing CPR (broken ribs are not uncommon), damage to the heart tissue after a heart attack and lack of oxygen supply to the brain all effect the quality of life one has after such an event. My man was frail and as much as it hurt at the time and pains me now, the right decision was made.

I left feeling absolutely gutted. W*hat a cruel world!* The doctors informed his next of kin and his wife and daughter came to pay their last respects, his wife was a little frail old lady helped in by her daughter who was quite an age herself, both displaying bloodshot eyes and puffy faces from prolonged tears. They were so grateful for everything I had done for them and their loved one, I expressed my condolences and accepted their gratitude but deep down felt I have failed my first test, a cardiac arrest and I was helpless.

Little did I know this was a feeling I would become accustomed to very quickly.

CHAPTER 2

THE UNEXPECTED

It was the start of October and the weather was finally cooling down. The ward was moderately busy, and I had beds 9 to 15 to care for. The day was going well, we were fully staffed. As the evening meal round approached, a lady was transferred to my ward from Accident and Emergency; she looked so frightened and frail. I had greeted her with a big smile (which I hope translated to my eyes as she couldn't see my mouth due to PPE (Personal Protection Equipment) now being mandatory). I gently held her hand as I introduced myself and my trainee nursing associate, Nikki. She had warmed to me straight away, her face had brightened, and a big smile had appeared across her wrinkled face, she began to tell me how she is going to die.

Great, a positive, happy optimist – just what I had needed! As I helped her into her bed and began the arduous task of completing the process to register her admission, she began to tell me all about her life and the mischief she has been up to. Now I am intrigued, no more talk of dying, just juicy stories, one of the very reasons I love caring for the elderly, they are full of mischief and gossip.

It started with her love of dancing. She told me how she met her husband, the love of her life, whilst they were at high school and were totally inseparable. He was a true romantic, however he had two left feet and would never have entertained the notion of dance classes. After his passing ten years ago, she had decided to join the local dance school on the high street, where she met the second love of her life, the one that had gotten away. Openly admitting that in high school she had been a bit of a flirt and fancied a lot of boys, holding a torch for one of the younger boys who happened to help run the dance school. She told me how her heart had skipped a beat as soon as she had clapped eyes on him, and when the opportunity arose to partner up with him, she thought all her Christmases had come at once. The chemistry was amazing, she described him as her Johnny Castle from the film *Dirty Dancing*, therefore she will now be known as Frances.

I was truly in awe of her. She was so passionate, forthcoming, and I could feel myself beam with happiness whenever I was around her, such confidence and commitment in her actions, she was a sure one to watch. Nothing was off limits, from wandering hands on the dance floor to sneaky snogs in the office, she didn't leave anything to the imagination, she was a truly happy soul, taking pride in her life achievements. She was a breath of fresh air.

Frances needed a lot of medication to offload the fluid surrounding her lungs so I had no option but to approach her with the notion of putting a catheter in. I could tell she was apprehensive, but my powers of persuasion won, and she agreed, a catheter it is. I gathered the kit, washed my hands, and popped some numbing gel in the area, she let out a childlike squeal.

"Oh, my goodness that was cold!" I sighed with relief, God only knew what she would have said given her previous stories and forthcomings. It had slipped it in rather easily and the fluid just flowed, giving her immediate release and comfort, and there it was, what I had been expecting, one could say patiently waiting for.

"There's been nothing in there for the past thirty years you know, will be like the Amazon rainforest." I had expected nothing else from Frances. I had giggled as I cleared up and turned to Frances jokingly.

"Frances, it's gone in your urethra, not your vagina, and I'm pretty sure nothing else should have been up there like, ever.' She burst out laughing.

"Told you it had been decades since I had any action anywhere." God, I love the elderly, so much life yet such little time left to share.

I could have sat there all evening listening to her stories, but the shift was ending, and she needed her rest, we parted our ways and I wished her a good night. This was definitely a story to tell the husband and kids when I got home, they would have loved Frances. She was everything I encompass in a grandma figure and a whole lot more.

*

It was the day after next when I returned on duty, and I so hoped that Frances would still be there waiting to tell more stories of her wonderful life and thankfully she was. Unfortunately, her heart was failing, and she was retaining fluid on her lungs, effecting her breathing and capacity to retain oxygen. She was on the maximum possible dosage of oxygen and consideration was given for anticipatory medications, medications usually given at end of life to ensure a peaceful passing. It was staggering how, having been so vibrant and full of life, in less than 48 hours she was now identified as end of life, a shell of what she was. Frances was so poorly, she was unable to speak and was very drowsy, my stomach dropped when I saw her, and my heart sank. She looked so different, she suddenly looked old and tired and (I'm sad to say) her age. I stroked her white head of hair and whispered to her.

"Everything'll be okay, Frances, you're in very safe hands." All she could manage was a weak smile of acknowledgment.

As the doctors did their rounds, they advised that priority was now comfort for Frances. Although death was not imminent, the family could visit. To my surprise, Frances didn't have family, she and her husband had tried for years for a baby, but it wasn't meant to be, all she had was her neighbour as her next of kin. I had called her neighbour who sounded very young and not what I was expecting, I advised of her friend's condition, her prognosis, and that visiting would be allowed for the time being.

That afternoon her friend came to visit, she looked the same age as me (early forties if you're wondering), and was ever so sweet, she had spoken very fondly of Frances, I couldn't help wondering if Frances had confided all her misdemeanours to her also. I could tell she was devastated and putting on a brave face so we discussed the prognosis and care being provided and the visiting rules due to Covid-

19, it was at that point she had asked if her boyfriend could come and visit. We had strict rules due to Covid and the policy was that only one family member, or next of kin, were allowed to visit and thinking that Frances had no other family she caught me off guard.

At first, I thought she meant her boyfriend, but she had in fact meant Frances' boyfriend, *she kept that little nugget to herself*, I thought. I've never been one to pry, but I couldn't help myself in this case.

"Of course, but I thought they were dance partners, and he was married?" The friend just chuckled.

"I bet *she* told you that."

"Well yes, she did," I had responded.

"Well, he was married, that bit was true, but the old dogs had been at it like rabbits for years!" Yes, Frances had obviously confided her misdemeanours to her also, we laughed together, and an immediate connection was formed. Nothing surprised me with Frances, but I must admit I was taken aback. My sweet little old Frances, a snog is one thing but doing the deed was another … good on her, age is just a number.

I watched as Frances' neighbour sat holding her hand, telling her how precious she was and that she could fight this. It's hard watching relatives and friends of patients, especially in end-of-life situations, they have so much hope and determination. That's one thing since becoming a nurse I forget about, we see so much death and heartache we just accept this as the norm, but everyone is individual with their own fight and lifetime of stories, with a world of love outside of the hospital. Sometimes I wish I didn't know as much as I do about human physiology, medical conditions, and prognosis as I feel like the grim reaper and the voice of doom when anyone asks about their ailments, sometimes it's best to say nothing at all, a sweet nod and complacent 'I am sure you will be fine'.

I spent the rest of the day caring for Frances making sure she was comfortable, clean, and presentable. By this point she's completely unconscious but I know she can hear me so as I checked on her catheter.

"Tomorrow's the day your Johnny Castle is visiting," I say sneakily, and, in that moment, I found myself imaging that he did actually look like Johnny and got all giddy. As I looked over, her eyes opened and she gave me the most flirtatious smirk.

No noise, just that smirk, it made my day, and I suddenly found myself also looking forward to tomorrow.

*

Reading through the following morning's handover, it was great to see that there had been no change in Frances for the worse. Apart from a few moans and groans when mobilising her, she had been given some extra PRNS (this is the acronym for medications as needed), to help with the pain and anxiety throughout the evening which in turn meant she was completely unresponsive, not what I had wished for as today was the day her boyfriend was coming to visit.

The ward was busy, and I had spent little quality time with Frances which as a nurse is always disheartening, but unfortunately comes with the territory. She didn't need me as much as my other patients, she was comfortable, clean, and being well looked after by the team.

It was after lunch when a very tall, well-presented, regal-looking gentleman approached the nursing station, and I knew immediately it was my Frances' Johnny Castle. I greeted him with a smile and completed all the test and trace paperwork as required. He was noticeably nervous, I reassured him that Frances was comfortable and in no pain when he confessed that she is the love of his life and that he felt so helpless. My heart warmed to him immediately. I totally got what Frances was referring to when she said he was the most endearing person one could ever meet.

My husband is forever telling me that I have a face that everyone wants to bare their soul to and today was no exception. Johnny's wife had dementia and had been in full-time care for the past five years, he visited her regularly but had said his goodbyes to her many years ago, he thought he would never love again until Frances walked into his dance studio, a true love story, ooh the goosebumps were 'goosing'. The look of love and admiration on his face was heart-rending. I had guided him slowly to her bed side, providing a chair for him to sit on.

"Talk to her, she can hear you," I encouraged him and as he began to speak, I had willed her to react, just a flicker, anything please, Frances. But there was nothing, she was a still as a statue, a corpse one might say. He spent his dedicated hour with her talking away, telling stories of the dancing team and their expeditions, how they have mastered the use of Facetime and were using this to share music and moves. His dedication to his wife and my lovely Frances were evident in his words, tenderness, and actions. As he says what he knows are his final goodbyes, the tears roll down his face, his shoulders drop.

"Thank you, Sarah," he says simply in his silky-smooth voice then silently leaves.

His grief struck me like I had been hit by a bus, I looked at my lovely lady and reminisce about how she made me feel when we first met, her mischievous smile and tales of past. I held her hand.

"Sleep tight my sweet," I whispered.

As my shift drew to an end I reflected on a surreal sort of day. I met my husband as I do after every shift and, as we take the short walk home, I offload my day. He loves hearing my stories.

"You tell a great story," he would always say.

*

Returning after my day off, I immediately popped my head straight round to check on my lovely Frances. To my surprise there she is, just as I had left her. There had been no change, just a plan to wean her oxygen down, so she may slip away peacefully, most likely today on my shift. I complete my medications round before I approached Frances as she wasn't going anywhere and her medications had been rationalised (that's the medical term for 'stopped') and she was receiving only comfort medications, usually strong pain relief and anti-anxiety mediations. I had approached, quietly, respectfully.

"Morning, my sweet, how are we today?" I said in a cheery voice, an immediate cold draft shuddered through my body as

Frances opened her eyes.

"I could murder a cup of tea."

What on earth just happened? I couldn't move, I just stood there like a deer stuck in headlights.

"Well," she reiterated, "can I have one?" I don't know what came over me. I know Boris said we can't hug, and I know the infection prevention control team would have me hung, drawn, and quartered, but I didn't care, my initial reaction was to give her a big hug, as tears struck my eyes with disbelief and shear excitement.

"Of course you can have a cup of tea, you can have anything you want!" My mind was spinning because she should be dead, I was thrilled! *What on earth had just happened?* I had called over my colleagues and the doctors who were all just as baffled. I checked her syringe driver (a device which delivers small amount of medication over 24 hours through a small subcutaneous needle) and there it was, her anticipatory medications hadn't been administered throughout the evening, the needle had become dislodged, leaving the medication to be absorbed into her dressings, an error on the night staff's part but I didn't care, it's a miracle and my lady was awake.

"I have so much to tell you!" I gasped. She looked confused, probably thought she had just had a few hours' sleep, clearly no idea what was happening.

The doctors examined and reviewed Frances and the decision was made, a complete turnaround and we were to start her medications again, she was a little miracle to say the least. Baffled by this miraculous recovery, Frances was on her way to getting better and I couldn't wait to tell her who I had met, how loved she was, and most importantly what a special lady she was. As soon as the opportunity presented itself, I sat down and had a good old natter. I told her about her neighbour visiting and spilling the beans on her, how the gorgeous Johnny Castle visited and how lucky she is to have such a caring and affectionate man.

"He's more than that you know," she swooned, "he is so strong and protective." We both agreed that she had a good thing going. "Use and abuse," she said, goodness knows what she had in store for him when she returned to full health, one could only imagine.

Unfortunately, he was unable to visit again as hospital regulations throughout Covid were that of end-of-life visiting, only which of course she wasn't any longer but it was only a matter of days before they were reunited once again and I was buzzing, as back on shift on her day of departure meant I got to be part of it. It's a great privilege if you get to share a patient's journey from start to finish.

Discharge day and we all lined up, the staff clapped and cheered as I wheeled her through the unit, our real-life miracle off to meet the man of her dreams and I was elated, like a teenager going on my first date. My Frances was so happy yet really couldn't grasp the fuss being made over her, I couldn't help but think that this could be the ending to a *Dirty Dancing* sequel!

It was very rare we had opportunities like this. We always prepared ourselves for the worst, not this time though, as a medical team we were beyond elated and we were loud and proud. It was a happy ending to what could have been a very different story.

As we approached the main entrance, there he was standing tall, hair immaculately tied back, his shirt neatly tucked in, with a bunch of flowers fit for a queen. I couldn't help it, I became all emotional, it was the ending dreams are made of, his big beaming smile as she approached him, they embraced, his tears flowed with happiness, my head was singing 'I've Had the Time of My Life' from the movie. He took over the reins of the wheelchair, he couldn't thank me enough, Frances waving like a mad woman with her flowers and off they went, I really hope they are still enjoying life to the full with one another.

This is why I love being a nurse, not everything is doom and gloom.

CHAPTER 3

IS THIS THE START?

It was mid-October 2020 and the media was in a frenzy with the threat of a second wave, staff were panicking as our unit was used for CPAP ('Continuous Positive Airway Pressure' device) during the first wave, leaving staff traumatised and exhausted. Since then, the trust had built a multimillion-pound ward in preparation, *so no need to worry, right?* Surely, they knew what they were doing, plan for the worst and hope for the best?

The ward was busy, and we had some very poorly patients. It's 10 a.m. and I had already been vomited and crapped on, but it was break time so off I jolly well went, soiled and all. As I had approached the break room I felt a sense of pending doom, my ward manager approached me and advised that I must go for urgent training on CPAP machines, she was very flustered and unusually assertive.

"It's not looking good!" she exclaims. *Never mind,* I thought to myself, I am having the day from hell so would welcome training, so naive as ever. Off I toddled to the coronary care unit where my fate awaited me.

There were a couple of nurses and a small, round sweaty

man hovering around a machine waiting for me, he cut my joyous morning dead in its track.

"Let's get this over with," he said promptly as soon as I had arrived. *Wow he definitely didn't work in healthcare*, despite some obvious hygiene issues he looked as though he should be in one of our beds, red blotchy skin, struggling for breath, he definitely didn't look overly healthy. My instincts were right, he was not a healthcare professional, he was there to demonstrate how the machines are setup, their functions, and how much each one costs – happy days! *Surely this was not the extent of the training?* I had no idea what fi02 or flow meant!? To my dismay, even to this day, that was the extent of the training. We all left baffled but on the plus side he did let us take pictures of the machine set up, because that will help. That and being reminded repeatedly of how much each machine had cost.

Living the dream once again.

I had my break and headed back to the ward; my manager eagerly awaited my return.

"How did it go? Would you be confident using the machines?" she asked.

"Err honestly no," was all I could muster.

"That's fine, I'll send a link of a video round that will help." *Will it though? Really?* I mean we all love a good video but all joking aside this was the literal extent of the training.

It was 2 p.m. and we get the call, apparently the new super multi-million-pound ward is not a viable option for CPAP machines as the oxygen tanks are too far away from it, therefore we now must try and discharge as many patients either home or to other wards in preparation for a second wave, and just like that my life was about to get spun into a whirlwind of Covid.

First, I needed to go and get mask fitted and do more training on how to don on and off (putting on all the required PPE and taking it off safely). PPE training lasted about 15 minutes (as time is precious), the fundamentals of it are basic.

"Keep everything on at all times, securing with tape where needed," the instructor says. Yep, that's how we roll in healthcare, you gotta love a bit of tape, it fixes everything, tape and paracetamol.

Mask fitting was a walk in the park with my overly round face, nothing was escaping there as they're so tight and suffocating, the rounder your face the safer you are, bonus! They put what can only be described a space suit helmet on, spray some disgusting mist in to see if you can taste or smell it, do a few dance moves, recite a few words, couple of arcane chants while waving a chicken foot at you.

"Still can't taste or smell anything? Great, you've passed!" Fat face won again.

*

After a quick break, it was suddenly 5 p.m., I had just received a patient from A&E and he wasn't looking too good, he was severely overloaded with fluid which was having a catastrophic impact on his breathing. Whether or not we manage to relocate everyone today, his admission needed to be completed so with the helping of my trusty Student Nurse Aisha, we completed his admission, took some swabs, and changed his leg dressing. The legs were the worst, they stunk with a pitting of green slop. Now I love a good wound, but pressure ulcers were the worst, give me blood and guts anytime. Unfortunately, the poor man didn't look good at all; he was on 10 litres of oxygen and scraping his saturation target of 94%, which raised alarm bells. I checked over his admission and he was deemed 'Low Covid risk' from the accident and emergency team. No symptoms apart from breathing difficulties which was put down to fluid retention in his lungs, seemed legit to me.

We had cracked on and trusted in the accident and emergency assessment. Bob was his name, and he was loving life and occupied himself by telling us about how he filed for divorce twice from his wife and kids during lockdown, even contacting a solicitor at one point.

"All they do is moan and eat. Moan and eat!" He kept saying it over and over, I couldn't help but chuckle as all *he* did was moan and eat. Nevertheless, he was a jolly man, he liked his food and drink, needless to say he was not impressed with his meagre supper but we did manage to get some odds and ends for him; some crackers and cheese, yogurt, orange juice, he soon perked up.

"You ladies know how to take care of a man." Was this his way of thanking us for our efforts? Men seem to think of this as a compliment but me and Aisha looked at each other, telepathically agreeing that this is a one off and outside of here he'd be getting it himself, as I am sure 'Mrs Bob' would agree.

Bob was really struggling with his mobility and shortness of breath and of course eventually nature took its course, and he needed a number 2 (I blamed the orange juice). Despite his protests there was no alternative except to bring the commode to his bedside for his use.

"I need a crap!" he virtually shouted.

"Totally get it," I replied, "but for your safety the commode is the only solution."

"Fine," he grunted, "bring the damned commode." My student nurse helped get him out of bed and onto the commode, he was so heavy and rigid it wasn't a pretty sight, but he kept himself positive by kindly stroking my back, yes stroking my back, and this was not the first or last time a patient had caressed my back.

"An unpleasant hazard of the job," I explained later to Aisha who was positively distraught by the thought. The lord answered our prayers, and he couldn't go (just a bit of noisy and very smelly wind), so we helped him back into bed, he was looking significantly worse than when he had arrived, so I have a look at his test results and boom! there it was.

He had tested positive for SARS-CoV-2, better known as the Coronavirus or 'Covid' for short.

I just froze. *How could this be? He was assessed as low risk!?* It was my first contact with a positive patient and to be far from my last. I had immediately informed the nurse in charge of the positive prognosis. Luckily Bob had been in no contact with anyone except for me and my student, Aisha, and had been confined to his bed space. He was removed immediately to the Covid ward (adeptly named Rainbow), protocols were put in place for cleaning and isolating the area, ensuring that the rest of patients' health and wellbeing were the key priority on the unit. These considerations were fantastic but the question that repeatedly ran through my mind was *what about us?*

"You'll be fine, you had your masks and gloves on," the nurse in charge reiterated from patient services. *Cheers, we all feel much better now.*

Not in the slightest, this was a very worrying time, and we all had the fear of giving a loved one Covid. Aisha was frantic, her father was immunosuppressed and would have a very poor prognosis if he were to get Covid, she was beside herself with worry and although I had tried to re-assure her that we did everything properly, i.e., wearing PPE, washing our hands until we nearly washed the skin off, she was nigh inconsolable. I booked her in for a rapid Covid-19 test and made sure she had somewhere to stay for the incubation period that was not at home with her father, she was so grateful for my efforts, but I couldn't help feeling responsible for her predicament. It was sod's law, it was her last shift of her placement with me as well, a gentle reminder that Covid doesn't make an appointment, follow any timetable, or discriminate.

That evening I found it hard to switch off, which is admittedly very unusual for me. I couldn't help but feel responsible for Aisha. She was so distressed; it was out of my hands, I did all I could, I would re-assure myself.

The day had been very daunting, this was this a small taster of what was to come. The morning couldn't come quick enough, as mad as it sounds, I was back on shift first thing and intrigued as to what was going to happen next.

The next day the ward area was almost empty. The CPAP machines had made an appearance overnight and we had our first Covid patient in a sealed off area. I really expected it to be Bob but it wasn't, it was a young chap who had been in a motorcycle accident two years previous which as a result had made him a left leg amputee, who was on day nine of Covid symptoms and was struggling to breath with poor oxygen saturations.

Harley was his name, and he was my first 'customer' of the day. The normal ratio for CPAP patients to nurses was to be ideally 1:1 (remember that ratio, it'll come in handy later), but stretching 2:1 due to their high dependency, however, luckily for Harley, today he had two nurses at his disposal. He was currently on maximum oxygen of 15 litres on a non-re-breath mask (basically a bag attached to the end of the mask thus ensuring he gets full amount), he was saturating poorly and had been transferred to us to trial some High Flow oxygen (this is a nasal option the machine had to offer).

"It's like sticking your head out of the car window going in excess of 70mph," is the term I would often use to describe the sensation to patients and no two ways about it, it's a ghastly experience.

I would describe Harley as a man's man, very well sculptured, dark hair with a well-manicured five o' clock shadow. He was very calm, relaxed, and showed little signs of anxiety as we advised him what we were going to do and attempt to change him over to the high flow oxygen therapy. The idea of this therapy is that it blows high pressure oxygen through the nose in an attempt to flood the lungs with oxygen (this is the flow setting). There are levels of oxygen concentration that can be titrated depending on the individual and their needs (this was the Fi02 setting).

It transpired that Harley had come off his motorbike two years prior and suffered horrendous injuries including a left leg amputation, he had also suffered facial injuries including fractured nose and cheek bones that caused general difficulties for him breathing through his nose which unfortunately meant he was unable to tolerate the High Flow Oxygen Therapy, so the alternative was to have the CPAP face mask. Before Harley's accident he had described himself as a very outgoing lad's lad, happily married with two boys and loving life as a motorbike mechanic. The accident had left him unable to work and was also the primary reason for the breakdown of his marriage, leaving him alone and scared. He'd had extensive rehabilitation both physically and mentally and was now in a good place. He'd won full custody of his boys six months prior and having a new love interest he felt his life was in a good place, so he was looking forward to what the future held.

A CPAP mask is like a normal oxygen mask, but thicker, more robust, and must be fitted tightly to the face, avoiding leakage. It has straps that fit over and around the head leaving little room for manoeuvring. The masks are very claustrophobic and (with the added pressure of high flow oxygen being pumped into them) a very unpleasant experience. The accident had left Harley with severe Post Traumatic Stress Disorder (otherwise known as PTSD) in addition to claustrophobia as his helmet had to be removed in pieces after the accident so he felt when we put the CPAP mask on, he was back there in the midst of his accident.

As harsh as it sounded, I had to put it to him straight; without the mask, his prognosis was poor and as the patients advocate, we had to be honest, the mask was sometimes the difference between living and dying. Despite his fears, he agreed to persist with the mask, with regular breaks and lots of hand holding. I can't describe the feeling of having a grown man hold your hand as you watch what feels to them as if they're suffocating. Begging you for help, you are their only lifeline in their eyes, the trust they have in you is overwhelming. Despite the awkwardness of holding the hand of a half-naked man, you must acknowledge that the only thing keeping them calm, and breathing, is you, their nurse, their trusted advisory. By grabbing me and holding on, Harley was saying to me *This is my life, now in your hands, please treat it well and do all you can for it.* An experience indescribable to those who have not experienced it.

When it came to handover to the night staff, Harley became very agitated, crying and begging me to stay on through the night, the fear in his eyes was evident, but all I could do was re-assure him. I had bent over him, stared at him intently with my clear blue eyes to ensure I had his full, undivided attention.

"You have one job, Harley, and that is to breathe." He stared for a moment then nodded in understanding. "Let us take care of the rest," I re-assured him. "You have one job and that is to breathe," I repeated. This was soon to become my tag line as it cuts through everything and conveys the single most important thing we need our patients to do.

Two days later and the ward was a different place, we were suddenly at capacity and with no staff, it was like a war zone! Staff were given a choice; they could stay with CPAP or *elect* to be redeployed. I understood that people have anxieties over Covid, some people have underlying health conditions, some people failed the mask fitting due to their slim, petite, little faces. Which left those with no excuse, they simply didn't want to do it and no-one encouraged them to do so, leaving those who did under staffed and fearful. Leaving my frustrations at the door I began my shift. I now had two patients, Harley who was in a state of despair and an older lady who hadn't quite ventured onto High Flow or CPAP just yet and is holding her own, which was just as well as Harley was demanding.

Harley wasn't progressing well, he was poorly and no longer tolerating the CPAP mask, he was barely holding his minimum target saturations and his anxiety was through the roof. He was exhausted and as I had approached him, he almost fell out the bed trying to grab my hand. He was so flustered, red like a tomato and breathless like a ninety-year-old who has smoked 60 a day and ran up ten flights of stairs. Harley was reaching the end of the road, he needed help with his urine bottle as he was so weak. As I helped him. my heart just broke. I know how hard this must have been for him, he was such an independent private soul. All he had to overcome and he's now back to having someone help him, although he didn't say this, he didn't need to as it was written all over his face, hanging his head almost in shame. My lady was independent and doing well so I had time to dedicate to Harley which was a great privilege and something I had been unable to do since qualifying as outside of Covid our ratio was 1:8.

Harley had received a message from his partner begging for a FaceTime call as his boys were missing him, but he really didn't want them seeing him like this. He had made the decision to have no face-to-face contact with them whilst in hospital, but a bit of gentle persuasion and he agreed it was time to let them know for now he was okay. Out came the comb for his hair, we popped a T shirt on (the machines make patients very hot so they're often naked down to their underwear). I removed the CPAP mask and popped on a standard non-re-breath mask and we were ready to go. "Stay with me please," he pleaded, "hold my hand."

"Of course," I had replied, I wasn't going anywhere.

He struggled to breath and speak to his boys, but they made him laugh more so at my expense, after all I looked like something out of a science fiction movie, all gowned and masked up, they were fascinated. It did Harley good seeing his boys, he had ended the call with a new-found enthusiasm, a reason for living and not giving up.

"I'm going to beat this, Sarah. I really am," he had told me. I squeezed his hand with a re-assuring smile which I hoped was reflected in my squinting eyes as that's all that's on show at this point. As I walked away, I had that little itch, the nurse's instinct that told me this wasn't going to end well. *Stay positive!* I re-assured myself.

It was a tough first day on frontline Covid. The Personal Protective Equipment (PPE) was just awful, it makes you sweat in places you shouldn't really sweat, the inability to have a drink on the ward, and the need to take everything off and put everything back on to have a quick wee is nauseating. The visors are so tight my head was pounding, and I had a deep red imprint on my head after wearing it for the shift. What a clip I was, my hair was stuck to my sweaty head, I had marks all over my face from my mask and my eyes are like two pushed in lumps of coal as if I was some kind of monstrous living snowwoman. As well as all that I had a banging headache from dehydration, but I was sure my husband would still have a smile for me (spoiler alert, he did!).

First job when I got home was shower and to order some safety goggles. I struggled to sleep that night because I could still feel the damn visor pressing against my temples, and the feeling of the mask suffocating me.

CHAPTER 4

AND SO, IT BEGINS

It was the start of November 2020 and in the blink of an eye I was back from two days off and the hospital was now code red, overnight patients had been shipped out to other hospitals and seventy five percent of all wards were now 'Dirty' (Covid) wards. With over 100 admissions in 36 hours, it was getting serious.

Harley had had a very bad night. He simply wasn't saturating well, and the decision had been made to move him to the intensive care unit. I was relieved for him because he was exhausted, time intubated (when patients are put in a state of sedation, allowing the machines to breathe for them) will give his body some desperately needed time to rest and recuperate.

Staffing was horrendous, patients are all very poorly, staff from all walks of life were deployed to help, with little knowledge and experience of caring for patients they were initially more of a hindrance than a help, it seemed like a losing battle, and it was only 11 a.m. I had three patients (you might have noticed the 1:1 and 2:1 ratio didn't last long), two patients on high flow nasal, who were tolerating it very well.

Then there was sweet Jane in her early 50s, currently tolerating the CPAP mask but she was making no improvements at all, but she was the perfect patient, the one everyone wants, doesn't want for anything and so grateful for everything. The saving grace for this day was I had the pleasure of our nursing associate, Nikki, with me for support. She was an amazing little pocket rocket, she just 'gets' patients' needs so well, she was on the ball, you never had to worry with her around. Having three patients with complex needs, continuous observations, with the potential to deteriorate at any time left little time for chit chat. Luckily for me I have the lovely, deployed helpers who are great for keeping patients entertained whilst me and Nikki got on with our nursing tasks.

It was the doctors' rounds, I loved the doctors' rounds when we were doing CPAP and Covid patients as nurses were now the fountain of all knowledge and the doctors relied on us more than ever. I had mastered the CPAP machine, totally got how to adjust flows and fi02's, but todays round was different, the mood was all 'doom and gloom', even my Geordie banter couldn't save us, we simply had no beds. Decisions needed to be made, rationalisation had begun.

We needed beds and Jane hadn't showed any signs of improving with the CPAP therapy, she was still struggling to maintain her saturations on the highest settings and was showing signs of fatigue. She desperately needed to go to intensive care for intubation and a rest. Despite all the commotion she was still smiling and trying her hardest to eat her breakfast.

"If I'd had this when I was younger, I could have lost a

few pound," she joked, I laughed.

"I could think of easier ways, like sewing up our mouths," I had replied and she tried to laugh with me, but ended up choking and struggling for breath, damn you Covid! Nothing is possible where it's concerned, not even a joke or simple laugh!

The discussions were had, Jane had refused to be transferred to intensive care for intubation and I got it, she had underlying health conditions with poor prognosis and believed that the bed be given to someone who has a fighting chance. It still didn't make it any easier. It's those words we hated to hear; 'Anticipatory medications', 'Make her comfortable'.

"Move to the side room so her family can see her through the window." My mind was reeling.

"What? Just like that we're giving up!"

"Yes, Sarah," the doctor said flatly, "we need the bed and machine, we'll wean the oxygen down once she has settled, and she should pass peacefully." To say I was shocked was an understatement. *Surely this had to be a joke.*

Unfortunately, it was not and was soon to become the reality of my role as a nurse living through the pandemic, priority being that of making people comfortable when all else had failed, it just didn't sit right with me at this point in time.

We moved Jane to the side room, she looked petrified yet calm, I felt every ounce of her fear.

"Your eyes speak a thousand words, Sarah," she said. I had given her hand a gentle squeeze and re-assured her we would do everything possible to make her comfortable, to which she nodded in approval. Once settled in the room, I advised her that her family were going to be contacted and could come to the window to see her, she was ecstatic, unfortunately the windows opened a little less than a foot, but enough to hold hands through.

The doctors contacted the family and advised of her wishes and the plan. Her husband, daughter, and son came to the window (Covid was so rampant, unknown and feared at this stage that the ward was in complete lockdown and we were told this is as close as we can safely allow families to say their goodbye), they begged us to have Jane change her mind and go to intensive care, they were clearly distressed and scared, but her decision was final. Jane's daughter passed through a picture of her grandsons, so innocent and unaware of what was happening in the world around them. We move Jane's bed as close to the window as possible, enough so they could hold hands. It was an awfully sad sight, I could feel myself breaking so I had made my excuses and left the room, heading straight for the doctor's office. There I was greeted through the door window by a very sympathetic doctor who agreed to let the family in for a very quick, discreet visit.

"Ensure it's a one off," he reiterated more than once, "and they must understand that the hospital holds no responsibility if they were to get Covid."

The family were overwhelmed at this news and obviously agreed to the terms. I had greeted them outside the unit, ensuring that they have full PPE, reiterated the risks of entering the department, ensured waivers and Track & Trace forms were completed. Once done we headed in. I was open and frank with the family, advising them that the priority was to make Jane comfortable with the aim of reducing her oxygen to see how she does. This wasn't full honesty but at that time we just didn't know, this whole scenario was new to everyone. The family showed a glimmer of hope.

"She's really strong you know! She'll surprise you."

There was nothing I wanted more at that point than to believe it be true. I explained how the CPAP machine was doing almost all of Jane's breathing for her, making her now wholly dependent on it, still their eyes glinted with hope. I took them in one at a time as agreed to see her. We tried to remove the CPAP mask, but she was unable to tolerate it, as noisy as it was it was a necessity and showed the family how poorly she had become. Tears poured down her family's faces as they encouraged her to fight.

"But she is strong," they kept saying to each other but strangely I noticed there wasn't a tear in sight from Jane. She told them how much she loved them, how proud she was of all of them and how if it was her time to leave this world, then so be it.

Her husband was the last to see her. He came out understandably distraught; her children, still in denial, encouraged him to be positive, he looked at me for backup.

"Tell them to say their goodbyes, Sarah. They need closure." My first thoughts were *I'm dying inside, barely holding it together myself, please don't ask this of me*, but I found the courage. I took their hands, one in each of mine and guided them back to the room.

"Go in together one last time, give your mum a big kiss

and tell her that you love her. She needs to know you're going to be okay." Tears had streamed down their faces as they walked in the room. Although adults, they are children, they're Jane's children. Like my children. It's heart-breaking but I know it's the right thing for them.

As I stood outside the room waiting for them, one of the healthcare assistants kindly reminded me that we were already breaking policy having visitors but to let two of them in the room at the same time is not acceptable. *Oh my god this is seriously not happening!* I smile sarcastically, not that she could tell the difference.

"Go away and think about what you've just said and if you feel it necessary then report it through the correct channels," I said through clenched teeth and glared at her. That sent her scurrying off (quick FYI, she did report it and I stood my ground with the backing of the team). I was livid! Who has the right to decide who and when people get the right to say goodbye to a loved one?

I re-united Jane's children with their father, they were so thankful for my efforts, I re-assured them that I would do everything possible to make sure she was comfortable and would have someone update them as and when anything changed.

As I returned to Jane, my nursing associate Nikki was pinning the picture of her grandsons up on the wall, it was heart-warming to think that they would be the last thing she saw in this life. It's came to the end of the shift and Jane asked for some ice cream.

"Sure!" I said and as I headed off to the kitchen, a doctor

stopped me in my tracks.

"How's the side room doing?" *Jesus, had everyone lost their sense of humanity?*

"Firstly, her name is Jane, and secondly she is wanting some ice cream."

"Ice cream? Are you serious? We need to relax her, we need the bed." *Was I hearing this?* I was furious! *So, no ice cream just medications,* I really wanted to punch him in the face.

"Ice cream first, and it's not up for debate." I brushed past him and continued to the kitchen.

Not letting my indiscretion in the corridor affect me, I headed positively back to Jane, she had just one spoonful of ice cream, it was all she could tolerate. As I drew up her medication it felt so wrong, yet so necessary, I was so torn, I even questioned whether this was the job for me? *Maybe I should bow out and join the rest of them on the other wards.* Then I go back to Jane, and I knew I was doing the right thing. She had lost this fight and it was my duty to make sure she passed comfortably with dignity.

My Ward Manager had to cover night shift as we had no staff. She was one of a kind, no other Ward Manager had stepped up to the plate like her, she was a true inspiration to everything we achieved through Covid. I handed over Jane to her, outlining the plan, she was clearly distraught and torn the same as I was but we both wanted what was best for Jane and that was to be comfortable, she promised to take good care of her and to keep her family informed. Now came the hard part, as me and Nikki entered the room Jane happily smiled at us both.

"Hope you ladies are going to have a big gin tonight for me."

"Of course we are, Jane, and tomorrow you can make us pay for having maybe one too many." Instinctively we both gave her a big hug. What an inspiration, she knew what was coming, but never let it show. As we walked up the corridor, Nikki started to cry inconsolably. I hugged her tight as I told her how amazing she is and we needed to believe that what we do is for the right reasons, even though sometimes it felt so unfair, it was the best for our patients, our duty of care.

Sadly, Jane passed away in the early hours of the following morning. Very peacefully and with my Ward Manager by her side.

We both found it hard to accept but were comforted by each other's woes.

*

It was busy day, and I had a new patient who was on High Flow Nasal (remember, head out of a car window, 70 miles per hour). He was, however, tolerating it well. Joe was his name, and he was in good spirits, we had a laugh and joked about the old 'Oliver Twist breakfast', he told me bread and butter with a sprinkle of sugar took him back to his youth.

"Mine too," I quipped, "but still yak!"

Health wise he was stable, not any worse but definitely not any better, just ticking along nicely.

He was comfortable in his chair just watching me

marching up and down the ward area.

"I don't know how you're so chubby, Sarah, with all the steps you do." I took it all in my stride, literally not pausing for a second as I responded.

"You should see me 'chub rub!'" His browed furrowed for a second then he roared with laughter as I joined in, the one-liners flowed, and he made my shifts fly by. The medication rounds were the best, he was prescribed a daily injection and he would scream "Ow! ow!" with such genuine sounding agony every time I administered it, much to the horror of other patients and staff. It became our thing. He wasn't really in any pain, he just loved to see everyone else's shocked faces and their reactions when I would announce it was their turn next. It was light-hearted fun, what you need when you are in the depth of death and despair day in and day out.

A week passed by and still no improvement or deterioration so the doctors decided to increase Joe's steroids to see if they could get him on his feet, despite the side effects of doing so the only alternative was to step him down to a normal ward which inevitably would mean a slow deterioration, and possibly an eventual death. He agreed.

"What's the worst that can happen? I turn into the terminator guy?"

"More like the Hulk," I replied and we laughed, he had such a full-on belly laugh that was so infectious, and I adored it, but the doctors didn't. They looked at us as though I should have been in a bed too, or even sectioned. *Smile and the world smiles with you,* I say.

I guessed they hadn't had much to joke and laugh about of

late. Thinking back, if I expressed everything that was going on in my head at these times, I don't think anyone would find fault in sectioning me. I have always been exceptionally good at disguising my true thoughts, probably for the best, I frighten myself sometimes.

The steroids did make Joe into the Hulk except for the turning green bit, he was up on his feet within days, causing mayhem. Although he still needed high-flow oxygen, he was finally improving, along with his new-found appetite. The 'Oliver Twist breakfasts' were no longer cutting it and his family were sending in an abundance of food for him, he was loving life, still screaming at his daily injections and antagonising other patients with his stories. He was such a great character, it would be a shame when he left us.

The day finally came when Joe was stepped down to a ward and my heart was full of appreciation for this great man, through it all he kept smiling and entertaining us, a great example of how rewarding being a nurse is. I kept an eagle eye on his progress on my days on shift, he was doing great, just waiting on the discharge team sorting home oxygen out for him.

Then just like that he was gone.

I checked up on him one morning and did a double take. There it was, the dreaded pop up: 'This patient is deceased, do you wish to continue?' My heart sank. Joe had died the early hours of that morning unexpectedly.

I am not one to get emotionally involved but this hit us all hard, especially me, he was supposed to be our good luck story, our Covid hero. I later found that his passing had been a painfully traumatising one. I couldn't help but think if he had stayed with us, it would have been different, but I also appreciate that his time had come for him to move on. Covid-19 doesn't just disappear, it lingers in the lungs and his had become suddenly plugged with mucous, basically suffocating him, the nurses tried to relieve the stress and pain, but it was too late my little 'Ow' man had passed, no longer exposed to the pains of this world.

His family sent a beautiful card and lots of lovely gifts with the words 'Tomorrow is never promised'. Never a truer word written.

CHAPTER 5

WE LAUGH AND WE CRY

Bed 11 was Margaret, our latest resident patient on CPAP, by the end of her stay I thought she was running the ward, she was practically a new staff member!

Margaret was very poorly, she was being nursed mostly in bed as her oxygen levels dropped to a dangerous level on mobilisation, however she refused a catheter and insisted on being assisted onto a commode. Margaret is a bariatric (large) patient and it takes at least two, sometimes three of us to get her to the edge of the bed but that's our job, that's what we are there for. However, some staff don't see it like that, protesting that she needs a catheter some refused to help, it's not a good working environment, but a common truth of the wards.

When a patient has Covid and they sit up right or stand from lying down, the position of the lungs changes, becoming tight and compact. Patients describe it as 'suffocating' and it's harrowing to witness the horror and sheer terror when someone experiences it. Margaret tended to panic, she was a full-on screamer and grabber all in one and to top it off she liked you to sit with her whilst she did her business. This bothered a lot of staff, but not me. As a nurse, you do what it takes to make your patients safe and comfortable, however on this one occasion I was even doubting myself.

I had returned on shift after an amazing two days off in a row and there she was, waiving and smiling at me throughout handover. Part of me was thinking, *Aw isn't that sweet,* the other, *How the hell is she still here?* Going with the latter I had no idea how she was still there, the side room was a revolving door, we were crying out for beds, we were rationalising oxygen and even putting an age limit on patients we were accepting, but she was still there? Targets for oxygen saturations (when we had enough oxygen) was 88-92%, Margaret, if she sat still fully concentrating on her breathing, could maintain 82%. However, when she mobilised, she was in the lower forties, she should've been an unconscious mess at this point, but she never was. The thing that set her apart from other patients was that she seemed for all intent and purposes physically fine, chatting, eating and drinking whilst taking the machines away with their constant red alarms going off. You would think she was on holiday.

Putting that aside, my patients for the day were Margaret who was stable apart from her dramatic mobilisation, tolerated High Flow/CPAP extremely well, and a chap in bed 12 who was an extremely obese gentleman in his early 40s who wasn't tolerating anything and simply wanted to die. His name was Leo, remember that.

The ying and the yang. Welcome to Covid-world.

I had approached Margaret for her morning medications and before I could say a word, she was at it.

"I haven't had a shit for over a week."

"… and morning to you too, Margaret," I respond with a smile, she laughed and continued as if I hadn't spoken.

"I have a lovely one brewing." *Been saving that for me I bet,* and her hysterical laugh confirmed my suspicions, she sure had been.

Margaret was a character. She had been on the ward for three weeks by this point which quite frankly was a miracle as most people last days, some even just hours. She thought she ran the show, breakfast served to her first, scheduled tea breaks, the works. To no surprise she was ready to off load. As she sat next to nurse's station, she had gotten into an unruly habit of not pressing her call bell and just shouting for assistance.

"Sarah I am ready for my special delivery!" Everyone looked at me as I nervously laughed.

"Coming darling," I had exclaimed and as I pulled the curtain round, she was beaming.

"I'm going to be half the woman I was when this is born." *Can't wait,* I thought cynically. *It's been a while since I was shat on.* She was mobilising better, taking only one or two of us to assist, but still screaming in panic and severely desaturating, the doctors had decided that this was her 'norm' and manageable for her.

She was perched on the commode, holding my hand as she normally did when she looked at me quizzically.

"Do you tell your kids and husband about things like this when you get home?"

"Of course, I don't!" This is what came out of my mouth

whereas in my head I am thinking *Are you for real, they live for this crack*. I sat holding her hand and it was clear she was in pain; I try to take the focus away by encouraging her to pretend that she is giving birth.

"Push and breathe," I say, "you've got this." In one last push, it's out! My goodness if only books had smell-a-vision. It was horrendous, it was a mix of a dodgy kebab and horse manure! Thank goodness for masks and safety glasses, they serve a magnificent dual purpose of blocking some smells, but they also disguise the look of disgust and nausea crumpling my face. As a nurse, it's the icing on a cake when a patient whispers those magical words after they have emptied their bowels:

"Can you clean me up? I can't reach." We smile.

"No problem," we usually say whilst silently praying *Please lord let it be a clean wipe*. It was; Jackpot! One wipe and we were done. We rejoiced in its arrival and christened it 'Judas' as it promised to be a beast but, in all reality, it barely filled the bowl.

As I removed the commode and its contents away from Margaret's bedside, I was greeted with a crowd of smirking faces and although we all have masks and visors on, I could see their eyes with their tell-tale 'squint' of a smile, watching me. As healthcare professionals, we believe that the curtains around a patient's bed are soundproof. News flash! They're not and as Margaret's bed is placed perfectly in front of the nurse's station, where the morning handovers are done for the doctors, it appears that everyone had the pleasure of my morning delivery just as much as me. Of course, it's the topic of conversation for the rest of the day and we all have a good giggle, although at my expense it makes a hard day that tiny bit easier.

Margaret was nothing short of a small miracle, she left the unit (bowels intact), after a four-week stay, discharged home a week later with home oxygen, hopefully doing well. Judas on the other hand went down the macerator, never to be seen again.

*

It was a new day and I had been assigned the 'side room' again. The side room was the one room on the ward that was a room, not just a bed with a curtain; a room which serves privacy and dignity to our dying patients.

In the room, there was a gentleman named Ben who I had only looked after a few days prior, he was doing so well, in the bay area, not one I would have pinned for the side room anytime soon. Guess that's one of the frightening realities of Covid, it has no boundaries, it does not discriminate, it affects everyone differently and there is no knowing what or who is next. Ben's family were at his bedside – his wife, son, and daughter – and although he was quite a few years older than myself, his children were roughly the same age as my own, my heart was already breaking, and I hadn't even spoke to them yet.

The handover was done and the plan was to reduce the oxygen slowly to assess Ben's reactions and ensure that he remained comfortable and was not in any distress. His family were aware of the plan and although apprehensive they understood and agreed, but throughout the morning he became a little unsettled, requiring more medications, so I agreed with the family to review that afternoon, before attempting to reduce his supply of oxygen.

The Sister and I reviewed the situation after lunch and agreed to reduce Ben's oxygen from 15 litres to 10 litres despite the doctors requesting it reduced to 3 litres via Nasal Cannula, a far too harsh a reduction which had been done previously, but we had the final say. We were the advocate for our patients, and we stood our ground, small reduction to 10 litres it was.

As we approached the room, I looked at the family. They were all exhausted, their eyes were puffy and red flowing with sadness and fear, this was going to be a tough one. I talked them through the plan to reduce the oxygen by five litres. I advised I would stay and ensure that Ben was still comfortable, once satisfied I would return to review in an hour's time. As I slowly reduced the oxygen, Ben hadn't flickered, a good sign that he was comfortable, the family were happy, and I left the room. Within minutes of leaving, the son came out of the room distraught.

"I think he's died!" he screamed. I turned immediately to see this man looking at me like a frightened little boy, eyes filled with tears ready to burst. I had got up immediately and took his hand and we headed back into the room. Ben's wife was sobbing into her hands and his daughter who was at the far side of the bed was begging her father to breathe.

She looked up at me.

"Sarah please." I moved to the far side where the daughter was, I checked for a pulse, there wasn't one, so I turned to his expectant family solemnly.

"He's taking his final breaths, I'm sorry."

A moment later Ben had stopped breathing, I removed the oxygen mask.

"It's time to say your final goodbyes," I said gently, almost a whisper. From nowhere the daughter had launched at me in desperation, pulling at my apron and gown.

"Please Sarah just five more minutes! I know he can make it, just give him five more minutes with oxygen!" My own heart was fully broken, I still don't know to this day where I got the strength from. I took her hands, bent down, gently eased her back into the chair she'd been sat in, and wiped her tears away as I took a deep, shuddering breath.

"Five minutes is going to make no difference," I said as gently as I could, she started to shake her head in protest, tears flowing again.

"Listen," I continued, again gently but firmly enough to get her attention, "he's still here and can still hear you, spend these last moments telling him how amazing he was and how much you love him." She looked at me, desperate, but she wasn't wailing anymore.

"No. No please no," she whimpered. I took her hands and squeezed them, gently lifting her to stand and I took her to her father's side.

"Tell him how lucky you are to have had him in your life. Tell him how much you love him. He can hear you." She fell in a heap across his chest with her mother's arms around her. As I left, her mother lifted her head and silently mouths the words, "Thank you."

As I had approached the door, the sister of the ward was stood there, tears streaming down her face. Everyone around the nurse's station just stared at me. I took the sister's hand and led her out of the side room as I closed the door, leaving the family to spend those last few minutes in privacy.

We hugged outside with the entirety of the unit staring at us, we didn't care. We're only human.

I went for a break whilst Ben's family said their goodbyes. Colleagues and patients commended me on my behaviour, I didn't feel like being commended, I felt like a heartless bitch. *Fuck Covid for what it's doing to people, to families!* I wanted to text my husband but already knew that if I offloaded too much on him it would make him worry, why spoil his day with my sorrow.

"It's life," I always say, a shit life but nevertheless, life.

I sat and reflected in our makeshift staff room which in reality was the fluid room with a patient table and plastic chair, the joys of working on a dirty unit. You couldn't congregate with the clean staff; it was uncomfortable and demeaning.

I had finished my break and as I left the break room, I heard a shout.

"Sarah!" As I turned, I saw Ben's daughter. She ran up to me, throwing her arms around me. "Thank you!" she exclaimed. "I'm so sorry if I hurt you." As I looked at her red face and bleary eyes, I put on what I hope is my bravest smile.

"You didn't hurt me, you were amazing. All of you were and your father was very lucky to have such beautiful people in his life."

Now Boris said at this point "We can't hug." But a running theme in this book will be that we didn't listen to Boris and hugging was all we had, a hug goes a great way to help healing, so we embraced. It was a heartfelt hug, the kind that makes you feel better. I watched as the family walked away, arms around one another with nothing more than a few carrier bags which symbolised the life of a man they loved, heart-breaking yet heart-warming. Such an amazing family now having to plan a life without their loved one.

Experiences like this was what inspired the writing of this book, the difference we make in people's lives are forever and vice versa, we don't get time to debrief as healthcare staff after traumatic situations like this, we should but we don't. We just don't have the time or in most cases the energy; hopefully, after reading this, people with connect with the importance of sharing.

*

After a patient passes, we do what is called 'Last Offices', we remove any foreign objects from a patient such as a cannulas or catheters, clean the patient meticulously and we prepare them for the porter to transport to the mortuary.

The family had asked me to take good care of Ben, their father and husband, therefore I insisted on completing his last offices. It's strange as everybody is different after passing, some people are cold, some hot, some look pale, some look yellow, and some look as if they are still alive and just sleeping. Ben looked pale and was very cold even though it had only been a matter of hours after his passing, he did however look so peaceful, exactly how you hope someone looks when passed. It reassures that you have done everything possible to ensure that they were comfortable and not in any pain.

As part of the infection protocol when a patient passes because of Covid, within the trust it was mandated that they are placed within a shroud, their face covered with an eco-pad and then placed in a sealed body bag attaching a notification of death certificated to the outer body bag. My first experience of doing this was soul destroying. As a student nurse, I had completed a placement in a hospice where we would never cover the heads of the passing and we would put a flower in their hands as a mark of respect. Covering a person's face seems so unnatural, don't get me wrong I know they have passed, no longer in any distress or pain, yet this simple act seemed to affect me the most – initially that is, as the time went on, I wasn't even aware that I was doing it, looking back now it feels surreal.

Once ready for the mortuary, we called the porters. 'Ward 11' we called it; I have no idea why it was the name given to all deceased on their final journey. The porters arrived, they refused to come onto the ward as they were afraid of Covid, despite the abundance of PPE that we were required to wear. They refused to enter the ward; it was down to the staff on the ward to transfer the patient from the bed to the gurney/trolley. I rallied the troops who were available; me, the sister, and our ward domestic. None of us had ever moved a body before and really underestimated the ingenuity it would take to do so.

"One, two, three and slide …" I had grunted as we heaved. Yep, not that easy, the body was now stuck between the bed and the gurney and oh my goodness he was heavy.

We shouted for help but there was none, the domestic held his head whilst the sister climbed on the bed.

"We're going to have to lift!" she said while we frantically fumbled away.

"Don't worry, my dear, you're in safe hands. I promise," I reassured the patient (we always treat and talk to the deceased as if they're alive, as a sign of respect). The three of us looked at each other. *What the hell were we doing?* If only Ben could see us now, having a great sense of humour he was definitely having a good old chuckle at our expense.

"Silly fools," he'd be saying.

Right on three we lifted again, but he just didn't move, he was literally too heavy for us, and we couldn't even roll him, he was completely wedged in, and we were beginning to feel the strain on our arms and backs, but we didn't give up, how could we? I grabbed a chair and stood on it so I had some height, the sister was already high on the bed and with all our might we lifted and yes! He moved, just enough for us to pull him onto the gurney. With a huge sigh of relief and sense of satisfaction we had made him comfortable and handed him over to the porters, with a clear message.

"Sort it out," I demanded, "we can't be expected to do this every time." They just shrugged it off as though we were overreacting.

Later that day we found ourselves in the same situation, another gentleman had passed in the bay area. We thought we were more prepared as there were four of us this time; two either side.

"One, two, three and …" you guessed it; stuck between the bed and gurney again. *What on earth were we doing wrong?* It couldn't be that hard, we even used a slide sheet this time. A colleague and I climbed on the bed. We rolled the patient this time.

"One, two, three … lift!" I shout as the other two do like a slippery tablecloth manoeuvre and he is on the gurney, thank the lord.

This wasn't acceptable. I could feel the strain in my arms and back, my colleague was doubled in back pain, we filled incident forms in for the porters to be available on the unit. It doesn't go down well as I'm sure you can imagine but thankfully after our third attempt, they agree to wear the PPE and complete the transfers, not before we needed some ibuprofen and codeine to help with the aches and pains.

I had observed the porters transfer the next patient, the wait for which isn't too long because sadly our patients are starting to drop like flies. I was astounded. No magic, no super method, just 'One, two, three and …' and 'Fwoop', slide straight over, they looked at me like I was stupid. To be fair I felt like it.

"We kept on getting people stuck between the two," I had disclosed to the porter after I saw him perform his miracle.

"How on earth did you manage that?" one of them replied.

"I have no idea. Three in a row as well." They were now laughing as though I was joking, so I just laughed along as though I was too. *What on earth were we doing?*

Stuck or not we took good care of our living and passed. Yes, we may laugh about it, cry with anger and frustration, but sheer care and determination is what makes us stand out, we take the good with the bad.

CHAPTER 6

IT'S NOTHING PERSONAL

It was what I had anticipated and dreaded the most, a phone call from home telling me that someone in my family had Covid. Being from an enormous family it was inevitable that someone would eventually catch it, but it's never who you expect. I have a nephew who suffers from hypo plastic left heart syndrome (he literally has half a heart) and ever since he was born, we have always taken precautions to use hand gel, stay away when we were poorly, and Covid times were no different. My brother had him isolated and did everything to keep him safe and thankfully it worked, even when his other children caught Covid, my brother kept him safe.

My aunty was also very conscious about health and safety and followed the guidelines to the letter so when she took ill suddenly with Covid it was unexpected, very unexpected, almost impossible to believe.

As a nurse, you soon realise how much you know and how much you wish you didn't know, sure everyone in the family has a role; my husband is the family's IT technician, my brothers and dad are the electricians and I'd become the family's go-to medical person, much to my dismay. My family were almost 300 miles away in Newcastle asking questions. 'Will she be, okay?', 'Why are they doing this?', 'Why can't they do that?' I didn't have all the answers, but I knew this wasn't good. Only a few weeks into looking after patients with Covid, I knew what to expect and I hated that I knew. I'd try to remain positive, careful to not to give too much away, sending constant hugs and best wishes.

"Am I a bad person?" I ask my husband one night.

"No," he replied without hesitation. Of course he did, but it doesn't matter what he said, I felt so torn, I don't ever have the answers, but I am always close.

My brother thinks I am psychic, I tend to say or predict things and they just happen. Not the lottery numbers or anything like that, but just day to day things, it's been a gift for years and my family trust when I say something as it tends to happen. So, to reassure my family felt wrong. My husband knew my concerns and I felt bad enough confiding in him as he now carried my pain and burden, but not forgetting Covid doesn't discriminate, so although I think I knew, I really didn't.

Shifts were long and hard now and there was so much pain and suffering all around me, my patients were very poorly, at least one passed every shift. My family are the only thing that was carrying me through the days, and I'll be forever grateful to have had them at my side, but even then there is only so much they could take.

My daily routine was walking to work with my husband and our boisterous Dachshund Kolbi. I loved it as he always 'bigged' me up for the day ahead (the husband that is, not the dog) and was always there when I finished to walk me home and be an ear for me to offload to. He lived and breathed every experience I had and remained by my side through it all. I am not an emotional person at work, despite how I feel on the inside I have a tough exterior; I sometimes think if people could read my mind, they would have me in a white coat or placed in one of the beds on the unit. Offloading is always good but knowing how much and who to confide in is key, my husband carried so much of my pain throughout my time on the Covid-19 unit and without him I am not sure I would have carried on as I did. When I talk to people about my experiences and the challenges, it's not for the glorification of what an amazing job I did, it's to raise awareness of how people suffered and the bravery that everyone displayed through challenging times, including my husband, my children, and my parents. Without their support and understanding I wouldn't be writing this today.

Learning to deal with grief from an early age makes you strong, having strong parents makes you strong, having the support and love from your own family makes you strong, but nothing makes you stronger than seeing the lengths your family go through to make sure you stay strong. I look back at my time caring for people with Covid, I recall my husband and children listening intently to the dramas of my day, the sorrow and sometimes tears in their eyes for my experiences and the glimmer of proudness for my achievements, its priceless and I will be forever in their debt. When my mam told me that my dad couldn't sleep for worrying about me, his little girl dealing with so much pain and suffering, he felt helpless, but he wasn't, it was the strength that he had shown and given me over the years which carried me through.

The strength my patients and families showed every day they fought this disease, dealing with the highs and lows, that's strength, a strength I wish I could have bottled and shared with the world.

*

There were differing trends in the patients that we treated; males in their forties being one of them, the first wave took out most of the older vulnerable people. We didn't have the resources and therefore the decision was made to put an age limit on who would qualify for the high-flow oxygen therapy which meant we saw a lot younger people through this second wave. This hit home for me as I held the hands of these men, they reminded me of my husband and brothers, big strong men, almost seen as invincible, now crying and begging me to help them breathe.

Then there was the 'Covid cough', once you hear it you will never un-hear it, I don't even think I can describe it, it's like a whooping cough with a squeaky toy sound to it. It looked like someone was suffocating, gasping likes it's their last breath as they are doing it. Grown men became fearful and helpless as I could only watch, distraught. I spent nights watching over my husband as he slept, terrified that he may one day catch it off me and be my next patient on the unit. It was such a hard time, looking back I don't know how I got through it.

Before being exposed to wave two, I was adamant that I would not get a vaccine.

"No way it's too soon," I'd say dismissively, "you don't know what the long-term effects would be and who knows what's in it?" A few weeks looking after Covid patients and I was ready to fight my way to the front of the queue, I didn't care if I grew two heads or died as a result, if I protected my family that's all that mattered. I still don't know what's in it or even if it's effective longer term, but we must have trust in the powers that be and play our part in preventing further deaths. I watch the news with all the anti-vaxers, and I am saddened by their accusations.

"Covid isn't real!" Err yes, it is, and until you have lived through it you wouldn't understand. I hope some of them pick up the urge to read this book and hopefully then will they see how real it is, how it has caused so much pain and suffering, denying people and families of such precious lives.

*

I'll never forget it, it was the 25th of November and the call I had been dreading came. As my phone rang, I looked blankly at the caller, 'Mam', and didn't want to answer, tears were running down my cheeks even before she spoke, I just knew it was bad. After weeks in intensive care, my aunty had sadly passed. Throughout her fight my aunty had my loving uncle and my cousins at her side, the thought of them by her bed with all the tubes and machines just willing her on as I did my patients was heart-rendering, but she was now at peace, no more pain or suffering yet little consolation to the family she has left behind. I am glad I am not on shift as this news hit me harder than I thought it would.

I let my ward manager know. She offered me time off for compassion, but I don't take it, we have little staff as it is and due to lockdown restrictions, I am unable to travel North to be with my family anyway, so I am better off caring for those who need me. I do take the opportunity to swap my shifts so I can attend the funeral via video link, with my husband and children by my side. I share a quick FaceTime with my parents before they head off to the funeral and they are beside themselves. So much heartache as my aunty was barely of pension age with so much still to give, a dearly loved wife, mother, and nanna.

As I sat on the sofa with my daughter by my side, my husband and son sat opposite us watching via their computer, we all wait silently, it's eerie as the video shows the hall with the alter and empty stairs and the dreaded curtains. The curtains once closed symbolise the final passing of life, I remember these as a teenager when attending my other aunty and Nanna's funerals. At the time, I was too young to appreciate their meaning but as the years passed with more funerals attended, I now do, and I dread it. It's an unbearable wait whilst my heart is breaking, part of me wants to see my family who I haven't seen for months, some several, but what comes with that is seeing their heartache and pain, I wasn't ready for that.

I see pain and heartache every day but its short lived, once a patient has passed and we comfort the family, it's for a short time and almost easy to step away from the situation once they leave. Today I was going to connect and experience the longevity of grief after someone passes with Covid. It was so cruel, only fifteen allowed to a funeral. How do you choose? Who do you choose? There will always be someone upset, it's so unfair.

There were sounds of shuffling and my family started to make their way to their seats, it was overwhelming. I immediately felt their loss and pain, shoulders and heads down as they jerked with tears, this was unimaginable torture. I'd turned and looked at my daughter, tears streamed down her pretty face, mine too as we hugged inconsolably. This was so hard. We watched as our family were united in grief, arms around each other, words of encouragement and love passed between them all. It was such a beautiful service, my aunty would have been so proud. As people were leaving, my mam and dad were right there in front of the camera and we screamed hysterically and willed them to look up, for no other reason just to let us know they were ok. It seems silly now as we FaceTime daily but, in that moment, we just wanted to know they were okay.

I messaged my uncle and cousins commending them on a beautiful service, they were thankful but so grief stricken. I dreaded the day I had to see them in person for I know, whilst I am in London hundreds of miles away, I am safe from the reality of living life after Covid.

It was months before I saw my uncle and cousins and I was a completely different person by then, after months of dealing with Covid, working sometimes five thirteen-hour shifts a week back-to-back, I had become harder than I ever thought possible. Don't get me wrong, I was caring, compassionate, and all things required of me, but I was different, my hard exterior was somewhat impenetrable. Although still offloading on an evening to my family, I was more careful as to the ins and outs of my day. I took on the role of 'Mother Teresa' my father would say, nothing seemed to phase me. Death? Exhaustion? Heartache? Nothing. I was like a ticking time bomb, waiting to finally crash but I never did, I imagined having a shower and screaming out all my anger and frustrations, but again it never happened. Covid had definitely changed me, some ways for the better, I was more patient and attentive, but on the flip side so dismissive and unattached. I am sure one day it will hit me when I am least expecting it, I just hope I am still surrounded by my family when it does.

CHAPTER 7

TIMES ARE CHANGING

It had been an eventful first three months as a qualified nurse; I had experienced more than some nurses would have in their entire career, but things were getting serious, oxygen levels were low and fights for beds were a real thing, decisions were being made and we were drowning.

Staffing levels were short and I had three patients, all very poorly, and as I received my handover, I see a little face staring and smiling intently at me, she looked so scared yet so happy. Her name was Sheila. Sheila was a lovely lady in her late forties, as young as this may sound for a Covid patient but this was what we were being faced with; younger, healthier people who had simply left it late from the onset of Covid symptoms before attending hospital and being admitted because they believed that they would 'get over it'. Sheila's sister was also in the hospital with Coronavirus, and they were on the same ward until Sheila got more poorly and had to be moved to our unit. What first drew me to Sheila was her smile, she was one of those patients that we all love, so grateful and appreciative of everything we do, however on the flipside they don't want to be a burden so don't let us know when things aren't going too well as a result.

Sheila had no interest in her prognosis or treatment and was more concerned about her sister, a few years older than her but less abled and a long sufferer of multiple sclerosis (MS). Sheila worked part time for the ministry and was a carer for her sister Sylvia.

"Please can you check how she is?" she asked me.

"Of course I can, Sheila, once I get you settled," I advised, at which point she gently touched my hand.

"No please just check on her. I am fine, I promise."

"You're not fine," I replied bluntly but I also knew she would not settle until I had done so. I brought the phone to Sheila's bedside and rang up to the ward. She was doing great.

"Recovering well and just as concerned about you!" I had exclaimed. Sheila immediately relaxed, her breathing improved and finally she was ready to listen to me.

I explained to Sheila that she wasn't making good progress and she needed help with her breathing, I explained the high-flow oxygen therapy to her, a nasal cannula is used to deliver oxygen at a high-speed, forcing oxygen to flow into the lungs, and although not as efficient as a full-face mask, it's a good starting point. Sheila was so apprehensive but after some gentle persuasion she was ready to give it a try. So, with tears in her eyes, I placed the straps around her head and as soon as the tubes entered the nostrils, she had started to panic. I was almost on the bed with her, I looked into her eyes and I held her hands, it looked like a birthing session.

"Breathe, just breathe. In and out, in and out," I had nodded with the rhythm of my words to affirm the positive, "you got this." With continued gentle encouragement and 30 minutes later, I was able to gently slide off the bed and carry on with my other patients. As I continued with my other patients, I could feel Sheila's eyes were transfixed on me, it felt a bit 'creepy', but she was so scared, so it is forgiven.

Breakfast time and Sheila was unable to eat because with the high flow of oxygen running through her nasal passage, she felt nauseous and as though she was choking, she really wasn't tolerating the high flow, so I suggested the full-face mask and reluctantly she agreed to give it a go. A full-face mask is the most effective way to deliver high-pressure oxygen into the lungs as it forces oxygen into them, increasing capacity, they are, however, very claustrophobic, suffocating, and only tolerable by few.

I had assistance from a colleague as we prepared to put the full-face mask on with straps covering the head to ensure that there is no break in the seal. Sheila started to shake and cry but without giving up we managed to get it on, again almost perched on the side of the bed I held her hand until she settled and relaxed, but it was clear she really wasn't doing too well.

I informed the doctors of my concerns once Sheila was settled.

"She's exhausted," I explained, "and the CPAP machine is on full capacity but it's not making that much difference in Sheila's oxygen saturations." It was time to admit defeat and for her own good, transfer her to the intensive care unit to be intubated and give her body a rest.

The doctors had agreed with me, as they have the conversation with Sheila I was there by her side, she was understandably distraught.

"Am I going to die, Sarah? Who will look after Sylvia?" I gave her hand a little squeeze.

"Don't you worry about, Sylvia. I'll be keeping a close eye on her for you, okay?" I responded and she nodded with a weary, childlike smile.

Transferring someone who is highly dependent on oxygen is dangerous and takes input from several disciplines, so I knew it was going to take a little while and seeing how distressed Sheila was, I arranged for a FaceTime call to her sister upstairs. Her sister was a mirror image and whilst I explained what was happening to Sheila and that she would be uncontactable while she rested, she was very calm and understanding. As I held the device for Sheila, she told her Sylvia that she loved her and they will be home soon, making plans for Christmas lunch and movies they are going to watch. I was suddenly overwhelmed with the realisation that Christmas was only four weeks away. I had barely given it a second thought yet these two had it all sorted.

"Please lord," I prayed, "let her make it."

It was my first experience of the intensive care unit in this hospital, and nothing could have prepared me for what I was about to witness. Sheila was all tubed up, doctors, porters, additional critical care staff were all present and we were on our way, it was approximately a three-minute transfer from our unit but the most stressful three minutes ever, constantly checking oxygen levels, heart rates and other vitals, it felt like something I'd seen on the TV. I stayed with Sheila the whole way, I had no choice as she had such a tight grip of my hand and her wide terror-filled eyes were still transfixed on me as we entered the intensive care unit to an eerie, unnerving quietness.

I looked around, fully aware, and so was Sheila as her grip got tighter and tighter, everyone was intubated. Beds, machines, wires, tubes in everyone, I was horrified. I had done time in an intensive care unit as a student on placement, but it was nothing like this, this is on the next level. Everyone was so panicked, I had no idea why Sheila was okay, she was stable so why the panic? They are all shouting instructions at each other.

"Err there is a patient here," I interrupted but nothing, everyone was too pre-occupied with the machine set up, so I made my focus Sheila.

"Jesus all this fuss over you, is there something you're not telling me?" I joked.

"Yes, I'm the daughter of the queen," she replied with a giggle.

"You're in good hands," I reassured her although given the kafuffle I was questioning leaving her here. *Have faith, Sarah*, I told myself, I knew it was for the best. Suddenly a little voice popped up from behind the bed.

"Before you go can you help put a catheter in?" It was one of the ICU nurses.

Sheila immediately piped up.

"Stick that in when I am asleep, please," she chuckled.

"I can pop it in if you like, Sheila, you won't be put to sleep immediately." She looked at me trustingly.

"Okay, as long as you do it." The nurse got all the equipment and when I talked Sheila through what I was about to do, she was mortified.

"I thought I was coming here for a sleep!"

"Sleep is the last resort," I said, "here we have another machine to try you on but first, let me get this catheter in and it will be one less thing to worry about."

"I haven't shaved for years mind," she exclaimed, "best get the garden shears out!" Then we nervously giggled, such a sweet endearing face, I hoped she was joking.

Right, all the gear and finally I had an idea! One thing was for sure, she hadn't shaved in decades. As I dug my way through, I ask Sheila for a gentle cough so I can identify her wee hole clearly.

"Oh my god what was that?!" As Sheila coughed, she had the biggest squirt of wee right in my face. Thank goodness for PPE! I popped my head up and Sheila was so red faced but became hysterical laughing when she saw my wet face, now she was dribbling wee everywhere and started choking on her mucus. I dropped everything as we rushed to sit her up.

"Deep breaths, come on, Sheila," I said calmly, but in my head, *I've killed her! Bloody Nora this cannot be happening!* and she unplugged ('coughed up' to you and me) a huge mucus lump and began breathing again. I blew out a deep breath.

"Told you I was funnier than Sarah Milligan!" I blurted, and she laughed softly.

"I am so sorry."

"There's nothing to be sorry about," I assured her, "it's one we'll definitely be telling over Christmas dinner for years to come!" I gave her a wink and then got back to business. The catheter was in and draining beautifully so I gave her a hug (another non-Boris hug). "See you soon, rest and take care."

On my way out I asked the nurses about my biker guy, Harley. She looked blankly at me.

"The amputee," I said, and they didn't need to reply. I knew just from the look on her face it wasn't good, he had passed the previous night. Whilst the team were extubating him, he had suffered a cardiac arrest, it was quick, and he wasn't in pain.

I walked slowly back to the ward, head bowed. I was devastated, we hadn't had any patients back we had sent to intensive care since Covid, please let Sheila be the first because it was just a one-way street at the moment.

*

I immediately changed my scrubs and mask, washed my goggles, and was ready to go again, everyone was intrigued what it was like up on intensive care, but I deflected the questions and changed the subject to tell them about my unwanted shower. It lightened the mood, and we all had a good laugh, even the patients were laughing at my expense again, but it didn't matter, laughing was good to see in such dire times.

Now down to two patients, I saw Doris waving madly at me, she had a full-face mask on, and she looks very flushed so, I rushed over.

"Are you ok?" She nodded and pointed to her mask. As I removed her mask, she took a deep, rattling breath.

"Can I have a catheter in?"

"But you already have one in?" I said and she laughed.

"I know!" The penny dropped, we laughed together and I gave her a short break from the CPAP mask and we talked about Christmas. She had so many children and grandchildren, I loved it, it really was the start of the festive season. I shared so many stories and dreams whilst looking after patients, some were just dreams but it's the connection at the time that makes them special.

One of the nurses from the male side came and asked for my help, I followed her around and her patient has passed, he was in the side room waiting for last offices. A lot, actually almost all the staff had a thing about doing last offices or being with the deceased on their own, but it had never bothered me. I am not afraid, my mam always says if they didn't hurt you when they were alive, they won't when they are dead. I recognised him straight away, I had looked after him a few shifts back, a jolly fellow, very rigid in his ways, always wanted his stockings on despite them being a death trap on the floors. He was one of our elderly patients, they were far and few these days with the average age of patients lately being forty to sixty years old.

"Right, first things first let's get those stockings off," I said and before thinking I grabbed his stockings, pulled them down from the knee, and low and behold it was like a snowstorm! Unfortunately, the snow was dry skin that had probably been in those stockings for weeks. *Oh my goodness, give me piss anytime!* It was awful!

"For the love of god!" I screamed. The nurse I was with just stood shell shocked, a healthcare assistant ran in to see what the commotion was.

"Is everything okay?" I couldn't help but laugh.

"Just getting in the Christmas spirit." She looked confused until I shook the remainder of the skin out of the stocking, and she ran out horrified.

"You're having a hell of a day!" the nurse I was with had exclaimed.

"All in an honest day's work," I responded and we laughed.

As we were washing and preparing the patient, don't ask me how or why, but the song 'Circle of Life' from *The Lion King* started playing in my head, I don't know the words fully, just the chorus, it's unusually comforting and makes the tasks ahead easier – singing, that is.

As we finished up, the emergency buzzer went off, so we ran. A young man in his early forties was unresponsive, he had been on the commode and felt faint. It took four of us to get him on the bed and we immediately applied his CPAP mask after whacking it up full volume, he became semi-conscious. The 'crash' (emergency response) team arrived and assessed him, no further action required, his oxygen saturations must have dropped whilst mobilising. We disagreed and stood our ground.

"He wasn't at his baseline; he was really off," we explained.

"Hourly observations then," the crash team lead demanded and off they went. Now I didn't know this patient, but he just didn't look right, call it a nurse's instinct, we have tendencies to just 'know' when our patients aren't well, and we usually didn't stop until we were heard.

I had to attend to my ladies, but we were all hands-on deck, looking out for the gentlemen when, with less than an hour of our shift, the emergency buzzer went off again but this time we knew who and where it was, so we ran to the male bay and the nurse is doing CPR on the same gentleman who'd had the previous episode. The call was put out while we took turns with chest compressions and, thankfully, he was revived and once again stable, he was so grateful for our efforts. The crash team couldn't do enough to help but apologies just weren't good enough, lessons were learnt, shame they had to be the hard way but nevertheless they were learnt. Unfortunately, there were no longer any beds in intensive care, they were at capacity. Our gentleman was still Covid positive and had to stay on our unit for the foreseeable but given our attention to detail it was the best place for him for now.

It had been a funny old day, I had witnessed the unbreakable bonds of sisters, I had been pissed and snowed on and I had learnt that I must stand my ground to protect the safety of patients, and that we are a damn good team on the unit.

As I had approached the main entrance, there he stood waiting, my knight in shining armour with his trusty canine steed, yep it was the husband and dog. As we walked home, I told him of my mishaps. He found it funny but also insisted that I take an extra-long shower when I got in!

CHAPTER 8

GOOD NEWS STORIES

It was the start of December and the lead up to Christmas, no team night out or celebrations though as the nation is once again in lockdown. I think the infection control team were working for Boris too as 'no decorations on the ward!', apparently they carry Covid!

I'm very aware that in writing and sharing my experiences there is a lot of doom and gloom, unfortunately this is true as there were many lows and very few highs, but the highs are to be celebrated and shared just as much.

*

You'll recall that a few chapters ago I referred to a gentleman I was caring for who was in his early forties and just wanted to die, well he somehow managed to fly completely under the radar and no longer wanted to die, quite the opposite in fact.

Leo was his name, he had originally come to us for oxygen therapy but was unable to tolerate it, with an abundance of underlying health conditions he was made palliative (end of life), and had been ticking along with his anticipatory medications, he had even had his implantable cardioverter defibrillator (ICD – an internal shocking mechanism to reboot the heart) turned off.

It was the first of four-night shifts, and I had no idea that this man was still alive let alone still on the ward! It was the early hours of the morning, and I was covering both areas of the unit whilst my colleagues took their breaks. The patient buzzer went off, as I went to investigate, I bumped into a very large, able-bodied gentleman and low and behold it was Leo. On his feet! With an empty jug in his hand!

"Can you fill this up please?" he asked.

"Of course," I stuttered, "as soon as I get that buzzer."

"Sorry, that's my buzzer," Leo confessed, he looked very sheepishly down at his other hand which had the buzzer in, lead in tow.

"Oh, my goodness have you been wrecking the joint?" I quipped.

"I'm so sorry I don't know what happened."

"Oh, it's fine," I reassured him, "happens all the time." While we walked back to his bed, I watched him walk and I was amazed. He had lost a substantial amount of weight and was looking good for it. When we got back to his bed, I popped the buzzer back into its wall socket and reset it then told Leo I'd be back in a minute with his water.

Now it was about 2 a.m., as I came back to his bed with a fresh jug of water, I somehow managed to stumble and spill the entire jug on the floor, wetting the side of his bed sheets.

"Shit!" I exclaimed, very quickly followed by "Sorry about my language". As I looked up, he was laughing his head off and, for that moment, a great weight lifted from my shoulders because it was such a fantastic sight to behold.

"Makes a change from me pissing the bed," he joked, and I had to laugh with him, because it did make a change.

When he was bed bound, he used the dreaded urine bottles, always spilling and dribbling over the sheets. I don't know what it was about urine bottles, but they were always spilling and overflowing.

"Designed by a man obviously!" I always joked. What was amazing about this time was that Leo was able to help me remake the bed, he actually had better hospital corners than me!

It was an unusually eerie and quiet night shift, everyone was behaving for a change, no alarming machines, very little moaning or coughing, all was good. Leo's theory on his miraculous recovery was that he had basically put himself in a state of a 'semi-coma', allowing his body to naturally recover. I couldn't disagree with his definition of it as a 'semi-coma', as for weeks he just slept and ate, barely moving off his bed, as we waited on him hand and foot.

Leo wasn't a bad patient, quite the opposite in fact. He always took his medications on time with no fuss and only buzzed when he needed assistance and otherwise generally just listened to his radio. I couldn't understand why he took up bed space on our unit as he didn't require or utilise the services we had on offer. This is one of the many things that I look back on and struggle to understand. We were moving people to the side room, almost accelerating the inevitable, yet here he was, steadily making little but excellent progress. I can't help but think if others had had this time would they be still with us today?

Leo's ICD was re-activated a few days later, he was eventually stepped down to a ward and left the hospital a few weeks later fit, healthy as could be, and just in time for Christmas.

*

Now, anyone who knows me will tell you how much I love Christmas! My husband jokingly refers to me as 'Mrs Claus' and by the time December comes around he's already rolled his eyes out of their sockets at my Christmas song serenades. Since a child it's the time of the year I live for, families together, no boundaries, just good old-fashioned joy and happiness. This year was going to be so different though, there would just be me, the husband, the children, and dog. No extended-family present swaps or Boxing Day at the parents, but that didn't matter, we had each other, a lot more than most had.

It was my last night shift of four in a row and I was exhausted, a lovely quiet first night and the most manic and depressing two which followed meant I was running on empty. I entered the ward and its chaos, another busy day with a few passings sadly; all beds were full and the machines running full throttle, I was not looking forward to it.

Handover was eventful, almost all patients were priority ones (sickest of the sick), except for one of my patients and even writing this now I am grinning. There she was sat upright in her bed, all proud of herself and waiting patiently for me to catch her eye.

"Sheila!" I had screamed (literally).

I couldn't believe it was her!

You see, Sheila was a first for me. In the two months of dealing with Covid, its victims, and seeing so many lose their lives and taking equally as many on the one-way trip to intensive care to be intubated, no-one had ever come back from the intensive care unit until Sheila.

It was magical and I was overwhelmed!

Unfortunately, I was assigned to the opposite side of the unit, but it didn't stop me catching up quickly, having a quick non-Boris hug in the interim. When you start a shift and it's chaotic, you tend to dread what the day and or night will bring, well this ended my string of night shifts as they started, nice and quietly, no dramas, no deaths, and no unwanted incidents.

It was a quick turnaround to day shift, due to staff shortages and sickness (staff were dropping like flies with exhaustion and stress-related illnesses) we were pulling in up to five shifts a week, and it still wasn't enough. I never make special requests, but I so wanted to look after Sheila as today was her birthday and not only did I want to be a part of it, I wanted to find out how Sylvia was doing, how she found intensive care and most importantly get her sorted for home.

My special request was granted, and it didn't disappoint, Sylvia had been discharged weeks prior and their mum had moved in to help. This was great news as the sisters and their mum had had a very fractured relationship so some good was to come out of it all. That afternoon I had hunted down the unit iPad and we FaceTimed Sylvia and her mum and I got a shock when I saw how similar Sylvia was to Sheila, their mum was just another slightly older version of them with shoulder-length silver hair, she even had the cow's lick they both had in their fringes.

It was amazing to witness and experience their mum saying she was going to stay with them over Christmas, you would have never known that they hadn't spoke for over ten years prior. Suddenly it had been decided that Sheila was to be discharged home that day. Ooh but we were waiting for a special delivery from her mum and sister, it was out for delivery up until 10 p.m. that night. I made a promise to Sheila that if it came before my shift ended, I would drop it at her home if she was okay with that. She was overwhelmed and agreed.

Tea-time and Sheila's transport had arrived. She looked so apprehensive and scared but with a gentle bit of reassurance, a couple of non-Boris hugs, and she was wheeled off the unit. We were so overwhelmed and proud, even if our patients made it to discharge, we never witnessed it as they were stepped down to a ward prior, it was great to see it for ourselves. Sheila's delivery came after my shift, I asked the night staff to put it to one side and I would take it the following day.

The following day I walked into our changing rooms which was the size of large closest with a tiny shower area and a very thin door to a cramped loo. Clocking the shower area where we hung our coats, I noticed a large box, immediately I knew it was for Sheila. It was a huge balloon – no I didn't open it, I googled the company name on the side. I rang Sheila and advised that her delivery had arrived and that I would drop it off after my shift, despite her protests she finally gave in and agreed. I wished the day away, I was super excited to see where Sheila lived and hoped she had settled back into home.

My son picked me up after my shift and Sheila's house was literally fifteen minutes from the hospital. The box was huge, I even had to put the seats down in the back of our Nissan Juke. I carried the box which was twice as big as me to a lovely, terraced house, I didn't even need to check the door number as I instantly identified it to be Sheila's. Ceramic ornaments surrounded the door, moons, stars, there were boot planters at the foot of the gate and the little patio area in front of the downstairs window housed two wooden chairs, it was enchanting to see. I could just imagine the two of them sitting outside putting the world to rights in the warmer months.

I knocked quietly on the door, a few moments passed then Sheila answered, she looked tired but well. I popped the box down, she just stood there staring aghast.

"I wouldn't have recognised you in the street, you look so different without all the gowns and things on." I think it was a compliment, well I took it as one!

"How's your mum?" I had asked Sheila, eagerly hinting to see them, but it was not to be, they were both in bed because even though it was only 9 p.m. the day had been exciting and taken its toll on them. Sheila presented me with a big poinsettia (Christmas plant), tears rolled down her face.

"I owe you everything."

"You owe me nothing, Sheila, you're the hero in this story, not me," I responded admirably.

Patients can be very appreciative of the care that we provide as nurses, but the truth of the matter is that they make a difference to us as well. Sheila, her sister, and mum puts everything in perspective, yes life's tough, the pandemic is shit, but it's also a great healer, it has given people time to appreciate what they have and some the opportunity to make much needed changes.

I have always been taught never to take life for granted, if anything screams this, it's now. Life is the most valuable asset we all have and if it takes a pandemic to show you this then so be it, take it as a positive, a second chance.

*

It is the week before Christmas and although things are not the same, I still have some festive spirit left in me, singing 'Jingle Bells' and 'Rudolph the Red Nosed Reindeer' completely out of tune and the patients are loving my vibes. A gentleman is stepped down from intensive care and – oh my god, he looked like Father Christmas!

"Ho, ho, ho!" I chanted as I approached him, and he laughed. He had been in intensive care for three weeks, two of them intubated, he was ready for a makeover, or wash at the very least.

"Can you give me a shave, but not a wet one?" were his first words (he obviously didn't appreciate the Father Christmas look!). I explained that we have an electric shaver, but I had no idea how much charge the battery had left in it but what was the worst that could happen? I started with blunted disposal scissors to try and take the length off before I shaved and it had worked a treat, he looked twenty years younger (but sadly no more Santa-like). Well done me. Then he wanted to push his luck.

"Fancy doing my head?" he said suddenly.

"Why not, what's the worst that could happen?" I'll tell you the worst thing that could of and did happen, the bloody battery died! The shaver started choking, spluttering and sticking, at which point I knew it was going to run out of battery, it was literally pulling the hairs out one by one before it died completely.

I kid you not when I say he had an almost perfect 5 cm square of hair left on the side of this head above his left ear! Luckily, he found it as hilarious as I did.

"Okay come on then, finish the rest," he said, flicking a thumb at his baldly temple. I looked at him, down at my hand, and realised that there was no charge for the shaver and nowhere had one. I rang nearly every ward in the hospital, nothing. As I was on the phone, I kept looking at this square of hair on the side of his head. *What was I going to do? There we go, let's make a situation worse, here come the doctors on their round, oh my god they are loving it.* However, I wasn't. Yes, it was funny (and luckily Santa was seeing the funny side as well), but it looked horrendous!

Suddenly an epiphany! The theatres have electric razors, our cardiology theatres have one, I had used it, but we weren't allowed in. I decided to take one for the team and in super stealth mode I 'nipped' in, grabbed the spare razor, did the business, cleaned and sanitised it thoroughly, and put it back before anyone noticed. I was now a true hero, he looked amazing, no thanks to my dodgy tools and even dodgier barbering skills. But it's never left me, even weeks after we laughed and laughed about it, these things only ever happened to me.

That afternoon he had his first FaceTime in three weeks with his son, given his appearance in intensive care he had refused the opportunity to FaceTime him, believing he was going to beat this he patiently bided his time. It was a great experience to witness and be part of and just a gentle reminder that being a nurse and nursing through the pandemic wasn't all bad, yes traumatising, but not bad.

CHAPTER 9

NEW YEAR, NEW YOU

I was at home watching the BBC news and a photograph of a very attractive lady in her early fifties flashed on the TV as in the background we heard the presenter talking to someone. The photograph was soon replaced by a live video feed of someone who looks like the lady in the photograph, but a much younger version of her. Leona Avci was being interviewed and explaining to the presenter that she and her family were non-believers, but she is now educating people on how real Covid is and how it can affect everyone.

"It doesn't discriminate," she proclaimed, and never a truer word spoken. As the interview drew to a close, the photograph was shown again and at a second viewing it hit me, I pointed at the screen and turned to my husband and children, gobsmacked.

"I know her!"

2 weeks earlier ...

I was one of the lucky ones and managed a few days off at Christmas, I appreciated it more so than ever, I would love to say that I spent my days off well but, in all honesty, I was exhausted and just took the time to spend with the family.

My first day back and of course it was eventful. It wasn't even 8.30 a.m. (an hour into my shift) and I was being screamed at for being a racist, if there is one thing I am not, a racist is one of them. Part of the admission process is to ask the question of any religious needs and beliefs, just so we are aware and can make any adjustments because of potential dietary needs etc. My lady who is named Diana, Diana Avci, and she doesn't appreciate this question as being from abroad she believed it to be unnecessary and intrusive, I had apologised and advised of the process we must follow, she didn't have to answer and so chose to decline, which I fully respected.

Having dealt with the public for years I soon learnt that the best thing to do in these heated situations was to remove yourself, let them calm down, and return in time. Little less than half an hour later Diana pressed her buzzer, apprehensive as I was, I needed to put her on the high-flow oxygen therapy, nasal or CPAP mask as it was apparent she desperately needed this.

Looking at Diana waving frantically in her chair I noticed her shoulder-length jet-black hair, not a strand out of place, beautifully applied make up on her olive-toned skin, she looked amazing. I had not paid that much attention to her appearance earlier on in the morning as she was hysterical, but she was beautiful, aged in her early fifties she looked ten years younger. It was obvious she'd had some enhancements on her face, including a lot of Botox filler. I approached with caution, offering my assistance and got the last thing I expected: an apology for her earlier behaviour. Diana had contacted her friend who worked for the consulate or other official body who had told her I was doing my job and confirming my reasons for the questions. An apology wasn't needed then or now, she was scared, and she knew she was very poorly, I finalised her admission and we began talking about her previous experiences.

Her son had been born long overdue and suffered brain damage at birth and although mild, she was his full-time career and she so needed to be at home with him, her daughter was on holiday abroad and didn't believe in Covid, it was her eldest son who had forced her to come to hospital after she collapsed at their family home.

I explained the high-flow oxygen therapy to her (putting your head out of a car window at 70mph,) she was so apprehensive, but when we got to the idea of the face mask, she was clear.

"No."

"I'm sorry?" I had stuttered.

"No. No face mask, it'll interfere with ..." She gestured at her face (Botox). The thought had already crossed my mind. We agreed to try the nasal high flow before I popped it on, I let her feel the force on her hands and face so she would understand the force in which the oxygen was to flow, she was not convinced of its benefit or effectiveness but agreed.

Struggling for breath at first, she got the hang of it and was tolerating it well. *Yes!* I was onto a winner, or so I thought. Diana's x-rays showed that her lung capacity was very minimal, her lungs looked like candyfloss on a stick, like the ones you got at the fair, it was unanimously agreed that the nasal wasn't going to do anything to aid her recovery and she needed the CPAP mask to force the lungs open and almost blow that candyfloss away.

As the doctors advised Diana on her prognosis and the need for the face mask, she protested profusely.

"You don't know what you are doing, I have been here before!" The doctors looked at each other, frowning in confusion.

"You lot gave my son brain damage!" and then she threw another long stream of similar accusations. All the medical team could see was an aggressive patient blaming the world for her misfortunes, being awkward. In comparison, all I could see was a very frightened lady, not knowing what was happening, out of her comfort zone, desperate to get home to her family. So, I did what Sarah normally does, I stepped in, calmed the situation, took full responsibility for what was about the happen which caused Diana to diffuse almost instantaneously. It's a great accolade as a nurse as that's when you know you have your patients' trust.

As I had attempted to put the mask on Diana's face, I started to panic. I had totally underestimated how much filler she had in her face. The masks need to fit tightly, often causing sores on patients' noses and cheeks but unfortunately it's an unavoidable 'must' to ensure that no air gets out and guarantees the full effect. On the plus side, there was no leaks and although her face looked very squidgy and almost like putty when you put your fingers in and it oozes out of the rim of the tub, she was certainly getting 100% of what was flowing in.

We had agreed to try it for two hours on, thirty minutes off, I had watched on for those two hours fearing what she would look like when I removed the mask, we nurses discussed the possibility of whether it would disfigure the face. No time to wonder, the two hours were up and the timer she had set alarmed, waving drastically at me to go over. *For the love of God*, I prayed as we unclipped the mask, but it wasn't bad at first, just a little imprint on the skin which was normal, but it wore off after a few minutes, she was happyish and agreed to the two-on thirty-off for the rest of the day.

Now because I had a few days off at Christmas it meant I was working all the way through to the New Year, thus meaning I was in for the following four days back-to-back.

Diana's toleration for the face mask had worsened with the days, her face was sore, starting to show signs of disfigurement and her mask-wearing routine had become a complete opposite of what we originally agreed, now almost thirty minutes on, two hours off! She was progressively getting worse, but Diana continued to refuse a catheter and was growing weaker and weaker and was now unable to get on and off the commode without assistance and a lot of hand holding. Tomorrow was New Year's Eve and Diana's 56th Birthday.

As I walked through the main entrance of the hospital the next morning on New Year's Eve to start my shift, I noticed a tall young man, his head down, shoulders dropped with his puffed-out jacket clutching carrier bags in both his hands. I knew who he was on approach.

"David, I presume?" He was startled and confused.

"Yes, how do you know?"

"I'm Sarah, I'm the nurse looking after your mum. You look so much like her." He brightened slightly.

"Can I come with you and see her? It's her birthday today." My heart broke as I explained to him that unfortunately he couldn't, but I would take her presents down with me. He looked like I had just shot his dog in front of him, shattered all his dreams, I literally was the worst person in the world.

"Please," he begged, "I miss her, she's so poorly." I had gently reiterated my stance and took the bags from him.

"I will wait, and can you come back and tell me if she liked them?" Oh my, I so just wanted to say "No", but of course I didn't, how could I? He was a child in a man's body.

As I went to Diana's bedside singing 'Happy Birthday', I realised two things; firstly, she wasn't wearing her CPAP mask and secondly, she looked like absolute shit. I couldn't help myself.

"What on earth are you playing at?" She looked startled.

"It's my birthday!" She sneered defensively and I could feel my cheeks flush as my frustration-driven anger started to rise. I didn't care if she was the queen, she was slowly killing herself.

"How many times have we discussed keeping the mask on? It's literally the difference between living and dying!"

Now probably reading this you're thinking, *my god this is a bit harsh,* but no it's not, it was how it was, keeping that mask on was the difference between life or death with Covid patients. I had seen it time and time again.

"Look at the state of my face, it's all lumpy and blotchy!" Diana cried, pointing to herself and to be fair it had been three days of wearing the mask on and off which had become the stuff of nightmares, not Freddy Kruger nightmares, but near enough.

"Stop being so vain," I protested, "you're beautiful." By this time, me and Diana are the best of friends because despite us having a rough start we had a lot in common, we were both great parents and role models and we were both full of life and stories and the same dry sense of humour, but she knew I was being serious and put her mask back on immediately. I gave her the bags of gifts and told her I needed to go see David and let him know she was okay; she was devastated that he was so close but she was unable to see him.

"Wear the mask and it'll just be a matter of time," I re-enforced.

I hadn't even started my shift yet, as I had approached the reception I noticed another gentleman with David, a bit smaller but with the same dark hair and eyes and lovely olive-toned skin which cleared marked him as his brother. They were both eager to find out how their mother was doing. I was honest with them, I told them that it was likely she would be moved to intensive care as she was non-compliant with the mask and was frankly exhausted. Intensive care would give her body time to repair, but she had to agree to that. I could tell in their eyes they were devastated, not what they wanted to hear but hopefully they could persuade her to comply because on my way up to reception the night staff told me that she had removed the mask as soon as I left for the end of my shift the previous day and had refused to put it back on all night.

I advised the sons I would get the doctors to give an update after their morning rounds and headed back to the unit. A little later, the results were in: Diana was progressively getting worse, intensive care was her only option, well that or the side room. I wasn't sure I could go through another episode of Jane. Thankfully, with some gentle persuasion, Diana agreed to go to intensive care and be intubated to give her body time to rest. I had asked the doctors to update the sons.

It was after lunch and the mammoth task to transfer Diana to the intensive care unit was here. I held her hand as we went in the lifts, keeping a tight grip as we turned the corners of the corridors until we came to the doors of the unit. *Please don't be like it was last time, a load of lifeless bodies some on their front some face up, deadly silence and tubes everywhere*, I think to myself. Of course, it was just like that but for some reason seemed a hell of a lot worse, there were more bodies cramped in the smaller space, obvious that some had been in that state for a long time. I felt my stomach knot as we passed through to a space in the corner, it was chaotic like the last time but less frantic. Diana had looked at me, panic-stricken.

"Please don't leave me here, Sarah." She was beside herself, almost in child-like wide-eyed hysteria with fear. "Please Sarah please! I promise I'll wear the mask, I'll wear the mask!" I felt like a total twat as I turned to her

"It's passed mask-wearing time, Diana." Her face crumpled as she started to cry. "This is your last chance to come back from this." Harsh again? Totally agree but this is what Covid is doing to us, and we quickly learnt that sugar-coating doesn't work, and we must tell it how it is. People aren't listening, they're dying, and this shit is serious.

"Please! Please!" Diana continued to plead, and I felt terrible, but I had to detach my emotions. I re-assured her that she needed to listen to the nurses. I'd be waiting for her downstairs when she was better. As I walked away, I looked back to a vision which I remember like yesterday, still glamourous in a sense, her beautiful dark hair, perfect eyebrows and olive skin but a shell of the woman I met four days prior, a slight hand wave from us both and I was out of the doors and back to the unit.

Diana Avci's died days later. Her death from Covid had a profound effect on her daughter, now an advocate for the vaccine.

*

Despite the PPE from head to toe, vanity was a running theme on the unit.

I had been looking after a lovely gentleman for the last two days and placed directly opposite him was a very jolly chap, George shall be his name. George was one of the lucky ones and had a bed near a window. He was in his late forties, slightly obese, very short in height, with a very shiny baldy head and his wife Jeanette visited several times throughout the days. She would bring her camping chair, perch herself in the shrubbery and with about six inches of the window open she would sit and keep George company, it was a wonderful yet sad state of affairs.

"Better than nothing," she would shrug.

It was my third of four long days in a row and a busy one, with shortages in nurses due to exhaustion, sickness, and isolation, we were struggling, it was literally an 'all hands on deck' and 'eyes in the back of your head' type of day. A lady in the side room had passed and the porters had arrived to take her to ward 11 (the mortuary) and as a sign of respect we closed all patients curtains until they had left the unit. As I closed George's curtain, he looked up at me from his chair beside the bed.

"My turn next."

"Next for what?" I had asked.

"To go in the room of death." I was startled, had the patients given the side room a nick name? Did they all think this is what it was used for? Don't get me wrong, the name was very apt, but hearing it out loud, especially from a patient, had sent shivers down my spine.

"You're doing great, George! That room would have to get through me before it got to you." He smiled sadly and looked down, he truly believed he was next, so I gave him a little smile (well a squint of the eyes) and closed his curtains.

His words troubled me, I told the sister and nurse who I was working with of his woes, and they didn't flinch or appeared shocked. *Was I missing something?* How had we got to the point where patients knew that a move to the side room would be their final journey? Although this was true, the fact that it appeared to be common knowledge didn't sit well with me.

The porters had left with their cargo, and we began to

open the curtains to plod on with the rest of our shift, the days were now getting monotonous; document patient's vitals, give them a break from the machines, administer medications, sit holding hands while telling them to breathe. I'm sure you get the picture; it was wearing us all down. The unit had no television, just a few radios with poor signal and while I loved to sing throughout my days, I only ever know choruses with the wrong words and I'm always out of tune but despite that it was enough to put smiles on everyone's faces. The patients and staff loved it.

"Every ward needs a Geordie nurse," they would say, an accolade I still wear with pride.

There's one song I actually know the words to.

"If you're happy and you know it, clap your hands!" Well, that and 'Happy Birthday', so the ward got that quite often! Everyone usually joined in except for a few disgruntled customers and it was a little bit of light-hearted entertainment. They say laughter is a great medicine but unfortunately for patients with Covid it could be more detrimental, as my patient starts choking with laughing which is easily solved; just a mucus plug, up it came and back down again.

"You'll kill us all off with your singing, Sarah!" said George on various occasions.

"At least you would die happy as long as you're clapping," I would respond, he would just laugh at me. It was true though, my singing could be the end for someone.

Jeanette was at the window passing through her daily batch of goodies for him and the staff. As I headed over, I saw tears running down her face. George's hands were holding hers through the tiny opening, she was pleading with him not to give up.

"What's going on here?" I insisted in a masterful tone.

"He's just exhausted, Sarah," Jeanette said, "and he thinks it's nearly his time for 'Death Room'." I hated the name they had given it.

"The 'side room'," I corrected, "and there'll be none of this." I turned to George. "You've got this!" I said with as much enthusiasm as I could muster at the time. At this point in time George was stable. Yes, he hadn't improved in the days that had passed but he was nowhere near ready for the side room. I finished my shift with a little rendition, "So long, farewell …" from the *Sound of Music*, as usual with the wrong lyrics and out of tune but they loved it, clapping and wishing me good night.

The following morning I felt good, it was the final day of four in a row, then a well-deserved two days off.

You got to be kidding me, for crying out loud what the hell had happened? As I walked down the corridor there was George's wife, Jeanette, talking to one of the evening nurses.

"Morning!" I said cheerfully, ensuring that everyone heard me, but when Jeanette turned to face me, I was stunned, she looked like she'd aged significantly overnight! George had taken the decision that he was too exhausted and wanted to go in the side room, he'd been presented no option to go to the intensive care unit first although Jeanette advised if it had of been he would have gone gladly. It had simply been a case that there were no beds at the inn so to say.

I was furious, although I had PPE from head to toe, everyone told me my eyes tell a thousand words, she grabbed my hand without me saying a word.

"It's okay, Sarah, we're both at peace with this." Well, I wasn't but I didn't let it show. His children had been to say their final goodbyes in the early hours of the morning (through the window of course), as George hadn't wanted then to see him before he was sedated. As Jeanette had requested, I agreed to be his nurse for the day and see that he passed peacefully. Goodness knows what he had told her, she seemed to think I was the best of best Grim Reaper the hospital had to offer!

I took a few minutes to read George's notes and took a deep, shuddering breath to compose myself before I went in to see him. This was hard as less than 12 hours prior I had told him he wasn't ready for this, now look at where we were. It didn't matter when I went into the room as he was already sedated, Jeanette sat holding his hand, long thick blonde hair covered most of her face, in full PPE from head to toe, she even had her gloves on. *How impersonal!* But it was for her own protection. I checked his syringe driver, he looked so peaceful and all I wanted, no, wished for, was that he would give me some 'back chat'. I didn't think it would be long before I could start to titrate (turn down) his oxygen as he was very unresponsive.

I advised Jeanette to let me know when she was ready for me to reduce the oxygen.

"Now," she immediately but calmly responded. *For the love of God, I had just started my shift, I wasn't prepared for this.* But it wasn't about me, so swallowing the big lump forming in my throat, I turned the oxygen down by five litres. Not a flicker. We sat patiently waiting for a response but nothing, everything stayed stable.

"Can you not do more?" Jeanette asked so I agreed to swap over to nasal and drop it to three litres and although this seemed like a big drop, it was what was recommended by the doctor's team. As I removed his mask and placed the nasal cannula on, I heard soft whimpering sobs from Jeanette. I didn't want to turn around. For the first time in this situation, I didn't feel prepared for the inevitable. I had felt vulnerable, distraught, and dismayed all at once and started swallowing repeatedly, rapidly. I gently stroked his face.

"This world's loss is a new world's gain." I don't know where this came from. I have never said, or thought it before, it had just slipped out.

"What a wonderful person you are," said a sobbing Jeanette behind me.

"Wonderful is a word I would use to describe George, not me." I had smiled at her. She just looked at me, tears flowing unchecked down her face as I gave her George's hand.

"Speak to him now, he can still hear you," I whisper. She had asked that I stay with them until he passed, this could be as quick as minutes or long as hours so I promised to remain as long as I can.

I stood back as Jeanette spoke to George about their life together, he was a deeply loved man. As I stood, with my heart breaking, admiring the courage she was showing, I remember thinking how calm and controlled she was and that if it were in her position how would I be? I hoped that I would be like her but in all honestly I think my tough exterior would crack and I would be a hysterical wreck. I hope I never get to be in Jeanette's position. George passed so peacefully and quickly, Jeanette left as we cleaned and prepared him for her children to come and say their goodbyes. It felt like a lifetime but must have only been thirty minutes later, we had washed and prepared George for his visitors, he looked so peaceful, his skin was a nice olive colour and his body still unnervingly warm, it was the best time for his family to say their final goodbyes.

As I had left the room, I asked the Junior Sister to do the final checks whilst I helped the family into their PPE. It was just mid-morning and I already felt like I had been hit by a bus. I took a deep breath, composed myself, and greeted George's son, daughter, and Jeanette from the unit entrance, they had clearly been crying, their faces all red and puffed.

"You were the lucky souls to have had George in your life," I said and they smiled proudly at this in agreement. I would say this often to families, not to make them feel good or honoured, but because it was true, as healthcare professionals, we get to know our patients inside and out, we experience them at their lowest point, they literally bare their soul to us, and we get to know what they're really like. As we had walked down the corridor, I could feel their tension building as they walked hand in hand, united as a family towards the side room. I stopped at the door to the room and as I had swung it open, I couldn't believe my eyes. Sat in full PPE, holding George's hand with one leg crossed over the other like Sharon Stone in *Fatal Attraction* sat the Junior Sister. She calmly stood up, still clasping George's hand in hers.

"He has been waiting for you," she gasped at the family, as she proclaimed her apologies for the family's loss, she left the room like a floating, godly like character. I was mortified and felt like apologising for the dramatics, but it wasn't appropriate, I left the family to say their final goodbyes and head off for my break, which was well overdue.

Breaks was one of my gripes within this trust, we got one hour and forty-five minutes unpaid breaks per twelve-and-a-half-hour day, whether we were unable to take them or not we didn't get paid, meaning that we only got paid for ten hours and forty-five minutes and as a result had to work seven shifts a fortnight the make up our contracted hours. In my previous trust, we had three breaks an hour unpaid split into two and a twenty-minute paid in the morning meaning we worked three weeks at three shifts and the fourth week would be a four-week shift. It didn't matter through the second wave as due to staff shortages we were working up to five shifts a week regardless. I opened the door to the break room; it was our old fluid room, but the fluid was now in the sister's office, and we had three chairs and table to our disposal, hard, plastic, almost made to be as uncomfortable as possible, great! I tried to rationalise what had just happened with the Junior Sister and just laughed it off.

"Bloody Sharon Stone eat your heart out!" I chuckled to myself. Inappropriate as it was, it had cheered me up.

By the time my break had finished, Jeanette had left and the final preparations had been made, porters had been called and George was off to ward 11. Deep breath and I was ready for my next patient.

I often reflect and think back to my time in Covid, I refer to myself as a 'heartless bitch', although I know I am not. I struggle to understand where the courage I displayed came from, in all honesty I blame my parents, through everything they battled in life they were amazingly strong and positive – cheers folks!

CHAPTER 10

MOTHER NATURE

It was the start of a night shift, one I volunteered for to help staffing. It was going to be a good night, I could tell just by which of my colleagues were on shift, the Surgical Sister from our Cardiology Unit was also covering a shift. I'd had the pleasure of working alongside her in my first few weeks of joining the trust and she was amazing. Full of positivity and knowledge so I felt safe on this shift, was that a weird thing to say? Not really, working through Covid I used to finish my days with, *thank God I still have my pin*. It had nothing to do with my capabilities, but it was the staffing, levels were just so short, you had so much responsibility and so many people pulling you in different directions, it was a breeding ground for mistakes. Tonight though, we had the A-Team.

Handover was dire, as usual I got the 'side room'. Staffing was low so I also got bed two and three which might not sound it, but it was a lot. Our guest in the side room was in the 'stable' stage; relaxed, not too sedated but enough to be classed as low maintenance, bed three was on the mend and due to be stepped down the following day and bed two was a lady recently moved from maternity for some oxygen therapy.

She'd only given birth hours prior to her fifth child. Anya was her name, and she was on day ten of Covid symptoms, with her recent deterioration she had given birth, an emergency caesarean, some thirty-four weeks into her pregnancy.

She had looked dreadful bless her, her oxygen saturations were abysmal, and she was struggling to breathe. With long black hair tied slickly back, she had a gaunt look about her, her sunken eyes were a piercing blue, with black circles surrounding them, the paleness of her skin did her no favours either. At the start of the pandemic there was enough organisation to have the males and females separated, however due to the strains on beds and other resources we were forced to mix the bay areas, although as we were now classed as a high-dependency unit it was in the trust policy for this to be allowed.

Anya understandably didn't appreciate the mix of sexes and insisted that her curtains always be closed but unfortunately I simply couldn't allow this either as she was very poorly, needed high-flow oxygen therapy, and close monitoring. So, we came to an agreement that I would perch myself between the opening of the curtains just enough that I could monitor her while keeping a close eye on my other patients.

It wouldn't have made a difference to me but could have an impact on her treatment when Anya advised that she was Jewish and would not endorse any blood transfusions, if she so needed to, I had reassured her that we fully respected her wishes and it was clearly documented on her records. Patients suffering from Covid often use their abdominal muscles to breathe as the chest capacity is so low which makes natural breathing almost impossible. Anya had recently had a caesarean-section so her abdominal muscles were compromised, and she was using every ounce of energy to breathe. As a result, her only option was to have the CPAP mask as this forced the lungs open to increase capacity rather than relying on the diaphragm and other muscles to draw air in.

Anya had agreed to this, we had placed the mask smoothly on, however she immediately struggled, started to panic and thrash around as though she was having a seizure/panic attack.

"Focus on me," I had said as I stared into her bright blue eyes with my own, deliberately matching her intensity. "You've got one job ... breathe," I would say persistently as she continued to stare at me. Minutes passed and she was still struggling so we called the hospital Night Doctor who prescribed a relaxant, it worked well but the affect was short lived. The next few hours Anya continued to struggle, and she had kept removing the mask herself, triggering the machine's alarm, until finally exhaustion kicked in and she fell asleep with it on thankfully. I had felt drained, on night shift we had to take our one-hour-forty-five-minute break in one go due to staff levels. I found it hard to take my full break on a night shift, I would put my earphones in and listen to the same playlist in the hope this would take my mind away from the patients and the unit. This night was no different, I had barely taken an hour's break as I couldn't rest as was usually the case. Tonight, though it was just as well because Anya had awoken and was struggling immensely. Patients get attached to a specific nurse and without me there when she awoke, she had become very scared and agitated, despite further medications she was not improving. She needed one on one support.

I had called the hospital-at-night team (this is a specialist crash team, but for the hospital at night), now it was not as though they didn't want to help, they covered the entire hospital, just the two team members, bouncing from one ward to another seeing the sickest of patients in a hospital that by this point is overrun and has all wards dedicated to the battle against Covid. They advised they would get to us as soon as they could. I had continued to monitor Anya, spending the next two hours holding her hand, encouraging her to breathe. She dosed in and out of sleep, there was nothing more I could have done but stay with her. The hospital-at-night eventually came but Anya was asleep, barely maintaining her saturations on the highest settings.

"She's stable," they advised, *great job!*

"Err no," I announced back, "that's not good enough, she's exhausted and needs to be intubated." They looked stunned but I knew Anya couldn't carry on like that and didn't want her to get to the 'point of no return', so I stood my ground. "I want Intensive Care to review." They had just looked at me like I was a spoilt brat. This is where who you work with makes a difference and the Sister, overhearing our conversation, approached and backed me up, a review was all we asked for, not a bed or transfer, just a review.

Given it was now 5 a.m. and only three hours left of our shift, it was imperative that this was to happen sooner rather than later, a change in staff could make all the difference. 'Lost in translation' would be the excuse so we demanded that she be reviewed within the next two hours given her persistent deterioration, surprisingly they had agreed. It was more like three hours when one of the Intensive Care

Consultants came down and it was a big fat 'Yes!' from me! I'd had dealings with this Consultant before, she was amazing and, most importantly, she was one of the good ones who had total respect for us nurses and our opinions. I had given a thorough handover, almost an hour-by-hour account of progress and deterioration, explained the caesarean and the impact this was having on her ability to breathe. She was in total agreement but not for a bed in the intensive care unit, given the fact that Anya had recently been through a caesarean, intubation would be ineffective. She needed to be transferred to another hospital in the trust and transferred over to an ECMO machine.

"What's that?" I asked and I was soon to know exactly what that was it was. ECMO (Extra Corpeal Membrane Oxygenation) was a machine which replaced the function of the heart and lungs, giving Anya the best chance of surviving and letting her body completely rest. It was a specialist machine and unavailable in our hospital, I had suddenly felt a sense of doom despite the consultant's protests that it was for the best.

"How long would she be unconscious for?" I had asked.

"At least two weeks to give her the best chance," she advised.

"But she's just given birth to her baby," I had protested.

"Yep, drastic solution, I know," the Consultant confirmed, "but a one that's needed."

The consultant explained to Anya what was needed, and she was understandably distraught but understood. My shift was coming to end but I couldn't leave her. It was agreed that she was to be given more anti-anxiety drugs to put her in a state of calmness for transfer and I stayed with her until she was almost unresponsive. It was a dangerous transfer, but the risks were far outweighed by the need. It was an emergency call with no time for her family to say their goodbyes, not even by FaceTime, and just like that she was whisked away.

Anya spent four weeks on ECMO and a further two weeks recovering before she was able to go home and see her son for the first time. Her husband visited my unit with the biggest box of treats for the staff and the most heart-warming picture and thank you note from Anya and her son, Isaac. So, this tale had an excellent ending, but I couldn't help but think, *What if? What if I hadn't stood my ground? What if it had been a different night, where there were no Sisters to fight our corner? What if the consultant had been that of a less appreciative one?* I generally don't live my life thinking about 'What if's', I may think them, but we must go with what we decide in the moment and not second-guess ourselves. We had to hope for the best as we were in unprecedented times. Anya may have been my first encounter and the most complicated encounter of pregnancy in Covid, but it wasn't our last as we had a gentle flow of patients who had given birth whilst being infected and therefore needing oxygen therapy, thankfully all surviving. The hardest days where when we had to watch them connect with their baby in the freezing cold through the gap in the windows, thank goodness, the snow held off through these times.

*

It was a quick turnaround from my night to day shift. A Saturday morning early January 2021, I'd been allocated to the front of the unit, and it was busy, everyone was very poorly and as a result alarms were being triggered constantly. I had popped to the back of the unit (it was a segregated six bed part of the unit, usually how we split the males and females), it was there where the controlled drugs cupboard lived. I noticed immediately a large lady; long black afro hair as wild as you would care to imagine on the phone giving hell to whomever she was talking to.

"You fuckin no good!" she yelled. "I'm in er' ill, dying, and you're out there, on your fuckin PlayStation …" she had went on and on.

I had turned and asked the nurse who she was talking to, it was her husband, a non-believer who had caught Covid from going to his mates during lockdown and had passed it onto her. She wasn't on any high-flow therapy, just a standard non-re-breath mask, she'd had a comfortable night with no concerns. But she wasn't happy.

"Yeah, it was fuckin shithole when I—" It was as if someone had pointed God's universal remote at her and pressed 'Mute', her voice just stopped. The silence, broken by the gentle sound of her phone dropping to the ground, caused us to swing round to investigate. *Shit, she was out cold!* Her nurse had rushed to her bedside as I immediately ran back to the front for the crash trolley.

"Put the call out!" I had hailed the healthcare assistant. "Adult cardiac arrest!" Unfortunately, this was all taking place during our first of the scheduled breaks, leaving two nurses and a healthcare on the floor. I had turned quickly to the check the healthcare assistant.

"You okay keeping an eye on the eight patients here while I assist?"

She nodded decisively. "Err ... yep." And like that off she went. She was apprehensive but luckily the most competent we had. This is us at our best, a unit, quick and efficient. As I had approached the back bay, the nurse had started compressions, assisting with the defibrillation pads. I had heard the Calvary in the background rushing to get their PPE on. *Hurry!* I willed them in my thoughts. This lady was thirty-three years of age, the same age my aunty died of a heart attack when I was a teenager. I was in auto pilot, my mind was taking me back to my childhood. My actions were the opposite though as I continuously shout a series of instructions ...

"Clear and shock!" Nothing. I began to overtake the compressions (you're trained to give compressions very hard and very fast, so you must swap over to keep momentum effective as they quickly become exhausting to do because of their intensity) when people appeared from everywhere.

There were two of us managing this situation up until now the best we could, how we had been trained to the letter. We both stood back and let the Crash Team take over as we switched to our training, giving a handover, assisting with medications and anything else they required. It was not looking good for the patient. Second shock. Nothing.

"Stand back!" Third shock and ... yes! She was back in the room! Right, time to stabilise and by now there were more than several people assisting so I regressed back to the front of the unit to assist the poor healthcare who I had abandoned.

The machines at the front had been sounding off one by one all morning yet in the thirty minutes I had been absent not one had sounded, everyone was stable ... thank God for that. I still hadn't got my controlled drugs but the patient I had wanted them for was no longer experiencing pain, sleeping peacefully.

I had continued to dip from the front to the back as they stabilised the lady, her prognosis was poor, they intubated right there and then but the task to transfer her from the unit to intensive care was as risky as it got. The other two nurses wandered back from their breaks completely oblivious to the events that had unfolded, one offered to assist the team in the transfer whilst the rest pick up the rest of the unit. I was desperate for a break so I could have a much needed wee, but I would have to wait to even have a wee as it would mean the removal of all PPE and putting it back on again and there just wasn't the time. After what felt like ages, which in fact was only approximately thirty minutes, the nurse who assisted with the transfer returned in tears. You immediately think of the worst when you see a colleague in tears, I prayed in my head that she is just a drama queen. Well, she wasn't a drama queen, neither was the patient dead, she had however suffered a further cardiac arrest on arrival to the intensive care unit. Xenia was her name, we followed her progress throughout the day, she was eventually transferred to our sister hospital needing ECMO as my previous patient did, at this point I felt there was a pattern looming.

The intensive care units didn't use the same system as us for patient care. It was crazy, the only way we could get an update on how our patients were doing was by checking to see if they had had a dietician visit, the dreaded deceased flag popped up, or if we knew someone who was working up there we could ask them, not the most efficient way but needs must. The NHS focus is caring for the patient, not letting the wider NHS know how a patient is getting on.

As Xenia had been transferred to another hospital we had to wait until a family member updated us, which was very rare. We had very few patients step back down to us from intensive care, in fact we had more patients be stepped back *up* to us after we had stepped them down to other wards.

It had been a long dramatic shift and I was due back to do it all again the following day. I poured my heart out to my husband, leaving the update for my parents to another time. Xenia had been too close to past experiences, and I had become very aware the effects my tales were having on them. When I woke in the morning my husband looked exhausted, he had spent the night worrying about how the previous day's events had affected me. Well obviously they had, but not enough to disturb my sleep, exhaustion took good care of that. I have a gift to be able to 'turn off', not all the time but most of the time; fully understanding that he did not possess this gift, I still offloaded. How selfish he must think I am, I felt like the worst wife ever. He was so understanding throughout my time training to be a nurse and even more so as my time nursing through the pandemic, if anyone needed recognition for their efforts it was him and the other partners and families supporting healthcare workers through this time, they were also victims and heroes of damn Covid.

A new day on the ward and the night staff had experienced the most traumatic night, one which touched us all as nurses. We had a patient, a gentleman in his mid-forties, whose wife was a nurse in the intensive care unit, he had been with us for a week or so, she had been isolating at home (as was required then having been with someone who had tested positive for Covid), and she had only returned to the unit on shift. The early hours of that morning he had taken a turn for the worst and the decision was made to transfer him to the intensive care unit, his wife was on shift in ICU at the time, a terrible conflict of interest but the decision was made. He was a Filipino gentleman, privileged to come from such a supportive Filipino community within the hospital, he was known by almost everyone, he had never shown any signs of deterioration and had been 'plodding' along nicely, so the events that unfolded hit hard.

Whilst transferring from our bed to the intensive care bed, he had suffered a massive cardiac arrest that would take his life in front of his assisting wife. The hairs stood up on the back of my neck as the story unfolded as part of our handover. I felt physically sick as I thought of his poor wife, how she must have felt, he was barely an age. The events of the previous day swept over me, and I questioned if enough was enough. We were all clearly exhausted, the PPE we wore drained us daily, the emotions that we were going through and what we were witnessing was at its peak, these were young people with their whole lives ahead of them, would this ever end?

CHAPTER 11

ARE WE TURNING A CORNER?

November 09, 2020, 06:45 AM Eastern Standard Time

NEW YORK & MAINZ, GERMANY--(BUSINESS WIRE) --Pfizer Inc. (NYSE: PFE) and BioNTech SE (Nasdaq: BNTX) today announced their mRNA-based vaccine candidate, BNT162b2, against SARS-CoV-2 has demonstrated evidence of efficacy against COVID-19 in participants without prior evidence of SARS-CoV-2 infection, based on the first interim efficacy analysis conducted on November 8, 2020, by an external, independent Data Monitoring Committee (DMC) from the Phase 3 clinical study.

After discussion with the FDA, the companies recently elected to drop the 32-case interim analysis and conduct the first interim analysis at a minimum of 62 cases. Upon the conclusion of those discussions, the evaluable case count reached 94 and the DMC performed its first analysis on all cases. The case split between vaccinated individuals and those who received the placebo indicates a vaccine efficacy rate above 90%, at 7 days after the second dose. This means that protection is achieved 28 days after the initiation of the vaccination, which consists of a 2-dose schedule. As the study continues, the final vaccine efficacy percentage may vary. The DMC has not reported any serious safety concerns and recommends that the study continue to collect additional safety and efficacy data as planned. The data will be discussed with regulatory authorities worldwide.

"Today is a great day for science and humanity. The first set of results from our Phase 3 COVID-19 vaccine trial provides the initial evidence of our vaccine's ability to prevent COVID-19," said Dr. Albert Bourla, Pfizer Chairman and CEO. "We are reaching this critical milestone in our vaccine development program at a time when the world needs it most with infection rates setting new records, hospitals nearing over-capacity and economies struggling to reopen. With today's news, we are a significant step closer to providing people around the world with a much-needed breakthrough to help bring an end to this global health crisis. We look forward to sharing additional efficacy and safety data generated from thousands of participants in the coming weeks."

"I want to thank the thousands of people who volunteered to participate in the clinical trial, our academic collaborators and investigators at the study sites, and our colleagues and collaborators around the world who are dedicating their time to this crucial endeavour," added Bourla. "We could not have come this far without the tremendous commitment of everyone involved."

"The first interim analysis of our global Phase 3 study provides evidence that a vaccine may effectively prevent COVID-19. This is a victory for innovation, science and a global collaborative effort," said Prof. Ugur Sahin, BioNTech co-founder and CEO. "When we embarked on this journey 10 months ago this is what we aspired to

achieve. Especially today, while we are all in the midst of a second wave and many of us in lockdown, we appreciate even more how important this milestone is on our path towards ending this pandemic and for all of us to regain a sense of normality. We will continue to collect further data as the trial continues to enrol for a final analysis planned when a total of 164 confirmed COVID-19 cases have accrued. I would like to thank everyone who has contributed to make this important achievement possible."

Ten weeks later

It was mid-January 2021 and time to book my vaccine. Since the announcements and speculation of a potential vaccine since mid-June 2020, before I even qualified, I always took the stance that I would not get it. All the usual palaver.

"It's too soon!", "We don't even know what's in it!" And, and, and … On the 8[th of] December 2020, a ninety-year-old woman became the first person in the world to receive the Pfizer vaccine following its clinical approval, she hadn't turned into a zombie or grown two heads. All it took was a few shifts on Covid frontline in the NHS and I was ready for this bad boy.

Some of the nurses and HealthCare Assistants had received the vaccine before I had, all had had some sort of mild side effect. Some soldiered on, most took at least one day's sick leave as reported through the hospital as staffing levels moved to 'Critical', before now it was at 'Survivable'. Despite this we were encouraged to get the vaccine, which in effect was very brave of the Trust given its impact. I had decided to have mine after the first of a three-night shifts and it was scheduled for 8.30 a.m. so I didn't have long to wait. Everyone was so eager and excited, the mood in the waiting area was surreal, this was it! We were winning and the tide was about to turn! We really needed the boost at this stage, these were the darkest days of the pandemic for us, people were dying frequently, and we desperately needed something, anything, to give us a boost. Being a sceptic, I didn't believe it to be our saviour, I believed it to be a necessity for our mental health more than anything, even as a placebo it had seen the mood of the nation change almost overnight.

I'm not a wimp but it bloody hurt, and my arm went instantly dead, *what had I done?* I had done what was needed, my husband and family were relieved I had some sort of protection on the frontline. Two paracetamols and off to bed I trotted (this later became my catchphrase), three hours later I awoke with pins and needles down my arm and a prickly rash covering me from head to toe. *Bloody Nora what the hell was happening!?* A side effect, great! I took two antihistamines and went back to sleep. A few hours later I awoke once again, and I felt awful; my arm was sore, heavy, and I still had rashes covering the insides of my arms adjacent to my elbows. The thought of calling in sick left my mind as quick as it entered because we had no staff. I wasn't unwell I told myself, it's a side effect. *Have a word with yourself, Sarah, and get to work!*

Whilst working we had to wear full PPE including gowns, stocks on gowns were limited and we were receiving supplies from all over the world and as a result that night's gowns were the worst of the worst as they were made of a plastic material, the type that made us sweat more than usual. The machines made the Unit unbearably hot anyways and most patients lay or sat partially clothed or in their underwear as a result. Full PPE meant that we would sweat buckets, this gown would see us able to ring out our scrubs after an hour or so, not the most attractive thought.

That night saw the worst staffing levels I had witnessed yet. I was in the rear area on my own with four patients. The nurse who had decided she was in charge was sitting comfortably at the front with two other nurses, two Healthcare Assistants, and six patients between them. I asked for help, it didn't have to be a nurse, a healthcare would do.

"No I'm not taking patients tonight as we might get some more patients," she said. *What the actual hell!?* I thought. There were medications due, so I did my rounds and went back.

By now it was 10 p.m. and they were having an easy time up the front, so I approached her again.

"I *need* help, it's not safe for me to leave the bay. I need to go to the store cupboard and what not."

"Call and I will send someone to cover," came the blunt response. That was it, I'd had enough, they had five staff members and six patients to my one (me!) and four patients. I choose my words carefully.

"Provide me with additional support or I will report it as an incident for dangerous staffing levels."

"Do what you need to," she responded and as I walked away another experienced nurse approached me.

"Are you on your own at the back?"

"Yes. Yes, I am, and I'll be filling in an incident report on Nurse Carole for dangerous staffing levels when I get the chance." She looked bewildered as I walked away, thirty minutes later everyone was settled, medications done, toilet runs completed, and fingers crossed they were all stable. I began to write up an incident report when a little head popped around the corner, it was one of the Healthcare Assistants from the front.

"Carole says there is no need to do a report, I can stay with you."

"Ah that's great, thanks for your help and support," I said, but filled in the incident report anyway.

Now me and Carole had crossed paths a few months prior and, to put it bluntly, she was known to be a lazy little trout. By this time (it was almost 11 p.m.) I felt like shit, my arms were on fire, and I had just spent the last three hours breaking my back making sure my patients were safe.

On nights, we used to start breaks at midnight, overlapping them by an hour to ensure that there was at least two on the unit 'observing' and 'walking the floor', that night was no different. I never felt comfortable leaving a healthcare on the floor on their own, especially a healthcare who had never worked on CPAP, but this is how it was, it is what they had provided me with for cover. She had her break, I made sure she took her full allowance because the combination PPE and nights weren't for the faint hearted. It was my turn for a break, and I reluctantly go just for an hour. I gave the Healthcare Assistant my mobile number.

"Call me if you need anything." Then I headed to the charity room and put my music on for an hour. Music was my saviour throughout the second wave despite where or who I was with, I used this as my distraction and release. This still didn't help me with learning the words to any songs or imbue me with the ability to sing in tune, but it was my go-to, to destress.

I got lucky on that night, the healthcare was amazing, really 'switched on' and enthusiastic. The morning staff arrived for handover, they were dumbfounded to find that I had been allocated four patients on my own and one of the Junior Sisters was present and immediately aware as the incident report had been dropped in her in-box in the morning. I had not called out any names in my report, but it was pretty apparent who withheld the support. She took me to one side, checking that I was okay (of course I was, I survived with my pin intact), she re-assured me that this would be an isolated incident and would be taken seriously. It wasn't my intent to get anyone in trouble, but the superiority sometimes goes to people's head, and I'd like to say that this was just the case with Carole, but it wasn't, she was just as lazy twat who didn't like doing work (in my opinion of course). My main thought was to get this damn PPE off, I was soaked in sweat and my arms were on fire and I so needed my bed. I left for home and my husband was waiting outside, dog in tow, to greet me.

"You alright?" he asked.

"Yep, just need my bed." I didn't disclose my night-time antics that could wait for teatime after I had slept.

I've always been an inquisitive person.

"Nosey Parker!" my dad would say, tit for tat in my

opinion. Having a highly inquisitive nature doesn't bode well for nights as you feel as though you miss out on so much during the day, so I always ensure I get six hours sleep then I am up doing washing, cleaning, and preparing dinner. The next two night and days were no different. My arms settled during the days as I slept but the PPE really exacerbated it, it was not healing, if anything it was worsening with my rash inflamed and developing into blisters. Finally finished my three nights now, I needed to turn it round for one final day shift of the week, anyone who does nights and shift work will tell you changing from nights to days is a killer but to finish nights on a Thursday morning to then do a day shift on a Friday is torture, but that's how it was.

Friday Morning and I was sat in our makeshift staff room, this is outside the exclusion zone for PPE, so I was sat in my scrubs, no plastic gown, and my arms were horrendous, they were blisters, they hadn't broken down yet but were ready to any minute. The Ward Manager noticed them immediately.

"It's just a side effect of the jab," I told her, but she was having none of it and shook her head.

"I need you to go get a PCR Covid test and get to your GP straight away."

"Are you serious?" I asked.

"Yes, we've actually got more staff than patients at this point and we're being in a slight lull," she concluded. Vaccines had been going for seven weeks and already we were seeing its impact.

Test done, photographs of arms sent to GP, who also

advised a PCR test, prescribed steroids, and stronger antihistamines, I didn't feel good at all, sore arms aside I was exhausted. There'd been a ban on all annual leave in effect since this kicked off at the end of October, the extra shifts had caught up with me, I felt defeated. I picked my prescription up on the way home. I didn't tell my husband or kids that I was coming home, they would only panic, and oh boy I was right, firstly I am never sick and, secondly, I never get sent home from work. My husband sent me to bed, insisting I keep the bedroom door open in case anything untoward were to happen. I love my husband and children deeply and appreciated all their concerns, but I was absolutely fine. My PCR test was negative, and my arms were almost cleared within a couple of days which was just as well as I was due back on shift.

*

I had avoided the WhatsApp Nurses' group whilst I was on my days off. I always did, otherwise I would be inundated with updates, updates I really didn't want. It's the start of February and the ward is eerie, the side bay was empty, all the beds were made but it was empty, were we turning a corner? Nah of course not, well that wasn't true the patients weren't as poorly as they had been, but the staffing levels were terrible. After their first vaccine, almost a third of the unit staff had contracted Covid! Coincidence? Apparently so.

Referring to my previous chapters and giving non-Boris hugs, not forgetting these hugs were given short and quickly with full PPE on from head to toe, they were not the most personable of hugs but most just missed any sort of human contact or affection. There was a nurse, the vanity nurse

(Sharon Stone), she was sat on the edge of a patient's bed with her full body (still in full PPE from head to toe) straddled across his, one hand on each of his shoulders.

"What on earth is she doing?" I had asked one of the other nurses.

"He's a nervous wreck, she has been like that with him all night."

"That's a bit extreme," I had said, it was an Oscar-worthy performance she was giving.

"She'll get bloody Covid!" one of the healthcare assistants exclaimed. I have so much respect for this person but even I was questioning her methods. She came to me at handover; he was going to be my responsibility today. I knew that days were a lot different from nights and there was no way I was going to be able to devote this much attention to him, but there she was, my saving grace, my little nursing associate Nikki back from her university work, this day just got a whole lot better.

The first patient of the day was doing amazing, weaned down from her oxygen therapy she was ready to step down to a normal ward and only required a little bit assistance on mobilising, so she was a little dream. Second patient was the nervous, needy man. I left him with my Nikki whilst I had sorted my lady out, but it was now time to sort him out. Unable to tolerate the CPAP mask, the doctors agreed to him having the high-flow nasal cannula, although not as effective it was at least something. Lee was his name, he was a truck driver, had been for twenty years, he was in his early fifties but looked a bit older from continual exposure to the weather through his lorry window. He was slim which I thought was unusual for a trucker, mousey blonde hair thinning on the top, perfectly cut into a crew cut, his eyes dark brown, droopy and sad looking.

"Let's have a break from this mask," I had said and he appeared delighted, little did he know the next stop was high-flow nasal. I did my little talk ("...like sticking your head out of your truck window at 70mph, blah, blah, blah"). He found it amusing, until we put the mask on.

"I'm choking!" he cried but he wasn't, he was a bit of a drama queen, the fact that he had someone sit on top of him all night comforting him didn't help.

"Stay with me," I had said calmly, "hold my hands." As you would have read in my earlier chapters, I had no issue with holding hands, comforting people even when they were taking a crap, but this guy wanted someone at his side constantly. Having lived through the past four months with Covid patients, we appreciated how frightening this could be and how detrimental it was to people's mental health, so we made a contentious effort to ensure that we dedicate as much time to him as possible. It was my turn and he was flattering me with all the "You're amazing" and whatnot. He was so adamant that he was going to die of Covid, but truth be told he wasn't half as bad as we had seen, and I was quite positive on his prognosis.

"Time to put the mask on," I'd say, "let's blow those cobwebs from your lungs."

Covid lungs on an x-ray had a very distinctive look, like a load of cobwebs or candyfloss on a stick, they looked like if you blew hard enough, they would disappear. A doctor once described the oxygen masks as doing just that, they force the lungs open and increase the oxygen capacity, it allowed me to visualise and explain the 'oxygen blowing the cobwebs away' and healing patients. Lee had a repeat x-ray that morning which showed that he needed more dedicated time on the CPAP mask to just do that as his cobwebs/candy floss was very dense and needed the therapy desperately. He refused to put the mask on, he protested that he preferred the nasal cannula. I tried to explain that the nasal cannula just forces the flow of oxygen through the lungs, the mask was what he needed to beat this as they forced the lungs open, increasing capacity, but he refused. There was nothing we could do but respect his wishes. My shifts this week were one day in and one day off, it sounds horrendous but in essence wasn't that bad. I said my goodnights to Lee.

"Now behave and I'll see you in thirty-six hours," I said and he laughed.

"I'll be dead by then," he replied as I pulled the mask over his head.

"And stop the nonsense!" I chuckled before giving him a smile then for the evening.

As we sat down the following day for dinner, the BBC news was on. They were there filming throughout the pandemic, and there was Lee, telling the news about me, how I told him the nasal cannula was like '... sticking your head out of a window doing 70mph.' He was praising the unit no end, bless, it was good to see him on TV but after he finished his talking, the next screen appeared:

Lee died shortly after filming this; his family agreed for it to aired to show how quick things could change with Covid.

This just couldn't be true! What on earth had happened? I pushed it to the back of my mind, the morning would come quick enough, and I would find out for myself.

Straight in the next day and on a computer, I brought up Lee's records; ... *died peacefully and suddenly in his sleep.* I found the ward sister. Apparently, he did his interview in the morning full of beans and life as I had previously witnessed, fell asleep before lunch, and simply didn't wake. No pain, no cardiac arrest, he just passed peacefully. I had looked at his last x-rays taken that morning and you couldn't even see the outline of his lungs, it was just white on white cobwebs. *He should have kept the CPAP mask on, damn it!* Could I have done more? I did my best; we can't force patients, we are there to guide them and I had told him "Mask or die" in a passive, jovial way, but I meant it and never a truer word spoken.

I had to take a moment, I was deflated, defeated, and unusually upset, what a waste! 'Mask, breathe, eat, sleep, repeat', that's all that was needed.

*

The news had an agreement with the hospital and had been covering it since the first wave. I had only had brief encounters with them up until this point, but my goodness they were about to feel the wrath of Nurse Dodds.

The side room had become the 'norm', each morning we

would pop our head in to see who was there and this day was no different. It was the lovely Lynette, a lady who I had the pleasure of meeting a few weeks prior, she was in her early sixties, small and petite in stature, she had little beady eyes with a smile that would encompass her face in its entirety. Lynette had only been with us a short time, she had been doing well and had been stepped down to one of the other wards. This was not an unusual occurrence, we saw a lot of patients who had been stepped down (probably too prematurely) come back to us for further oxygen therapy but they very rarely ended up in the side room. Lynette had a daughter and a granddaughter who had been taking it in turns to be by her bedside over the past 48 hours. 48 hours was *very* unusual for a patient to last without oxygen therapy, but Lynette appeared to be an anomaly, she was a miracle, and absolute champ! The team were still adamant that this was an end-of-life situation, but I couldn't help but think Lynette was not ready to give up the fight. When patients are classified as end of life, as mentioned in previous chapters, their regular medications are stopped, we no longer monitor vital signs, and they are given medications to help them relax. I knew it was not the 'done thing', but I needed to know for my peace of mind, I slipped an oxygen saturations probe on her finger (monitors oxygen flowing in the blood stream), it wasn't good, but it certainly wasn't bad; 86%. We had been accepting less than that when oxygen supplies were low. I told the nurse in charge, who was bewildered at my actions but understood as to why I would check them, we both couldn't help but think what if she was a Covid miracle?

Looking back at this time in our journey, we were

desperate for some goodness. Just one little good news story to lift our over-exhausted and ove-emotional bodies. It was unfortunately not to be; as the hours went on, Lynette's colour became grey and her breathing slower, it was time for the granddaughter to come.

"Tell her to call you when she is at the main doors and I'll get her fitted for her PPE," I told Lynette's daughter, "and tell her to not to panic but be as quick as possible please." Lynette was at the final stages of life. I anxiously watched Lynette and the clock until the call arrived, as I approached the doors there were a young woman in her mid-twenties, a slightly older woman, probably late forties, and a young man also mid-twenties.

"Sophia?" I called as this was the name of the granddaughter and a young girl popped her head up, she was in her late teens.

"That's me," her voice was so broken and young my heart sank for her.

I had ushered her past the three overly excited persons blocking the doorway. As I was getting her fitted for her PPE, a voice interrupted.

"Do you have a moment?" It was the lady in her mid-forties, tall, with immaculate dark brown hair, face full of make-up and false nails only us nurses dreamed of.

"No," I had responded as politely as I could muster.

"It won't take much of your time. We've heard of a miracle lady in your side room, a Lynette Brown, we hear she is beating all odds and giving you lot a run for your money."

You couldn't write this shit! I thought in my head, this was not happening.

"I'm sorry but it's not appropriate," I had advised, "you should leave and speak to the Matron or Ward Manager."

"They know we are here," she pressed, "who do you think called us?" I looked at Sophia who at this point had her head down looking to the floor, tears streamed down her face, dropping on the floor. I felt my jaw clench and jut out as I spoke.

"This is NOT appropriate, please leave." The man accompanying the news lady piped up.

"We're the news team covering the hospital," he advised but at this point I didn't care who they were, I needed to get Sophia to her grandmother and out of this situation.

"You need to leave," I demanded, and as I turned and put my arm around Sophia to lead her away, the woman grabbed her arm, causing both of us to swing round.

"Are you her family? Can we come with you?" I was dumbstruck, I couldn't believe it! I pulled her arm away from Sophia's, I was seriously annoyed at this point.

"I won't ask you to leave again, before I call security," I growled, scowled, and turned our backs on them once again.

I ushered Sophia through the doors onto the unit, apologising profusely, it was of course up to the family if they would like news coverage of the events, but they didn't.

"Please Sarah," they begged, "make them disappear." I spoke to the Ward Sister who advised that I was to tell them to 'sling their hook' if I so wanted to. Oh my god I so wanted to, I marched straight back out the doors.

"The family want nothing to do with you so you need to leave immediately."

"Well if they change their minds—"

"Just leave, now!" I shouted. It was like something that would be scripted in a film, I was shocked and bewildered, had they no morals or empathy? It was obvious that Sophia was only a child, how dare they? Matron got wind of the dramas and she was fuming, she had told them the day prior it was inappropriate, this would not be end of it. She was a good matron, she did however look like Miss Trunchbull from Matilda with an Irish accent, she didn't suffer fools that was for sure.

Lynette was a strong lady, all in all she lasted fifty-one hours without oxygen therapy. Her family did not want to do a piece with the news, they were unforgiving in their approach, as was I, it was calloused and unnecessary.

CHAPTER 12

WE ALL HAVE OUR WEAKNESSES

Putting my disappointment behind me, it was a new day with new challenges.

Although I have said that Covid doesn't discriminate, there seemed to be a few patterns to the patients that we treated, with one being that of diabetes. High glucose levels over time can cause damage to the lining of small blood vessels, impeding circulation. The use of the steroid dexamethasone (used to treat patients with Covid 19) has a detrimental effect on the blood glucose levels in an individual, so when used with a patient with already diagnosed diabetes, blood sugar levels must be closely monitored, usually hourly.

My lady was no exception. Glynis was her name and eating was her game, this was a day shift to end all day shifts. I have always struggled with my weight and can empathise with patients to a certain point, but Glynis was topping the scales at twenty-six stone. She had been equipped with a bariatric bed and chair and needed the assistance of at least two of us on mobilisation, she was nowhere near the worst I had seen but was far from the best. I greeted her with a pleasant "Morning!" to be greeted with a face full of tears and snots. Glynis was not on a CPAP mask as her x-rays had identified that she hadn't needed this yet. She was, however, on the high-flow nasal cannula, which she was tolerating exceptionally well but she was crying as she was hungry and during handover the night staff had expressed their concerns with the constant need for food.

With her being monitored hourly for her blood sugars (which were exceptionally high), they had been reluctant to give her any more after a midnight feast of cheese, crackers, yogurt, and toast with jam. They had even gone to the extreme to moving her fresh juice (very high in natural sugars and not recommended at best of times for diabetes patients) from her bedside, in the hope of reducing her blood sugar levels – it had worked moderately.

Breakfast time and our usual catering assistant was unable to continue to work with us through the treatment of Covid patients due to her underlying health reasons, she had been replaced by Tyrone who was amazing with the patients, he was patient, courteous and had all the time in the world for them. It's not to say that the usual catering assistant was bad, but my goodness she lacked empathy and patience. If a patient was asleep or taking too long to decide what they wanted and place their order, they got whatever was easiest plus bread and jam, a cup of tea with milk for breakfast whether they liked it or not. Tyrone had a sense of health and well-being so when Glynis asked for four slices of bread, jam, honey, cornflakes, porridge, and a yogurt for her breakfast, he was not phased.

"Come on! A pretty lady like you doesn't need all that." He gave her two slices of toast with butter and some porridge. "Try that and if I have anything left after my rounds I'll pop back." A sly little wink to me and he went on his way.

Glynis was on the hourly blood glucose testing, it's a small prick on the inside of your finger to generate a splash of blood for the test and it bloody hurts! Patients like Glynis were used to these tests, their fingertips often purple and full of little prick marks, but it didn't faze them. Glynis was on regular intravenous drips titrating between insulin and glucose to try and get her blood sugars stable and it was one of the most time-consuming medication administrations known to me.

"For the love of God what are you doing!?" Yep, that was me shouting that from the nurse's station. Glynis had somehow managed to get half her body cocked over the bed rails, her white arse was showing full view, her ginger, frizzy hair drooped down her face and in her hands was a carton of fresh orange juice, she was gulping it like a mad woman before I could get to her and had it dripped all down her gown and bedding.

"I just needed a drink!" she protested.

"Then you should have just asked," I responded, this was not good, it had already been explained to her how fresh fruit juice is a definite 'No' given her high blood sugar levels.

"I just love it," was always her response.

"Well you can't love it in the afterlife," I shamefully responded and it was true! I had seen it time and time again over the past four months, people with diabetes had usually died because of Covid. I was becoming a pessimist, I'd never typically been all 'doom and gloom' but I was always being exposed to this situation and didn't appreciate it one bit. I was not alone as it was an ever more progressive trend within the team.

After a good wash, bed change, and fresh gown, Glynis agreed to spend some time out of bed and in the chair, a change of scenery was as exciting as it got the patients unable to move from their bed spaces due to the oxygen machines being hooked up to the supply in the wall, some in this state for weeks (no wonder they were going mad). We had printed out some crosswords and puzzles for the patients and the nurses took it in turn to get the free Metro paper daily for the patients. I am horrendous at crosswords and so was Glynis, so we decided to have a game of noughts and crosses, winner gets a biscuit – I thought my life was bad revolving round food, but poor Glynis was obsessed. Now 11 a.m. and I was losing the will, literally every time I turned my back Glynis was eating biscuits, fruit, anything she could get her hands on. Her blood sugar levels were through the roof and I had no idea where she was squirrelling all this food!

Doctor's rounds and they were less than impressed with Glynis, her excessive blood sugar levels and her recent x-ray is just as damning, so time for the CPAP mask, she most definitely won't be able to eat with that on! She didn't protest at all.

"If it's what I need," she said and we agreed to trial it two hours on, thirty minutes off. *Would I be luckily enough to get two hours of peace and quiet?* Of course not.

Thirty minutes in and, "I need a drink," she whimpered. Although the masks have humidification running through them, they did dry patients mouths but not usually thirty minutes in.

"Persist with it, Glynis," I had encouraged her but then the tears started. I didn't appreciate it when patients cried, understanding that it was just an emotion, I'm almost shamed to say that I'd grown quite passive in its effects after months of witnessing tears. Glynis was exhausted; she had spent most of the evening eating or moaning and it had been reported that she had had little to no sleep. It was time for a mid-morning nap one thought, I sat by her side and held her hand.

"Glynis do you trust me?" I asked.

"Of course!" she said.

"Well you have *one* job and that is to breathe." I sat holding her hand at her bedside whilst I completed my admin with my free hand and within fifteen minutes she was snoring like a baby. *Yes, this will do her the world of good*, I thought.

Glynis slept through lunch and it was pushing 3 p.m. in the afternoon by the time she woke, obviously starving, horrified at having missed the lunch rounds but already looked better for it. I got her lunch from the kitchen, a sandwich, fruit, and a yogurt. She was less than impressed but devoured it, she was back on the nasal cannula whilst she ate.

"Time to put the mask back on," I said as she finished, she tried to protest but after a few stern words she agreed.

"Two hours," she reiterated back to me.

"Yes, two hours," I agreed, holding two fingers up the polite way-round, "then it'll be dinner time." I was warming to Glynis, she wasn't as dramatic and demanding as she'd previously been portrayed, she was understandably scared, bored, and her coping mechanism was food. I'm sure we've all been guilty of that at some point. She was my only patient that day and it was re-assuring that I could dedicate time to her, our computers were on wheels (inappropriately nicknamed COW's), and it was no heart ache to complete the required administrative tasks at a patient's bedside, despite most liking to congregate at the nurse's station or in their little corners. Glynis had her iPad, she was happily playing bejewelled as I continued with my tasks. I was doing my handover notes and from nowhere the shrillest, piercing alarm went off, causing me to topple off the chair in fright! Luckily, I caught my fall and quickly looked up to Glynis now with her ginger locks neatly tied in a ponytail so we could get the mask on properly, her big brown eyes wide open in shock.

"I'm so sorry! Are you okay, Sarah?" she said, clearly embarrassed. *Was she taking the piss?* She'd only set an alarm for two hours! I picked myself up and laughed with her, it was funny, and no-one was harmed, well maybe my ego a bit but this is how it was to be, patients took what we said literally, two hours meant two hours.

Dinner time and Glynis is fed and watered once again, her blood sugar levels were still high but had remained steady throughout the day, so there was some progress made, that and only a few episodes of tears. I handed over my actions to the night staff, they hadn't had any experience of Glynis before but were confident she was in safe hands.

*

The following day I was back at the front, I had popped my head into Glynis on my way past, but she was sleeping and allegedly night staff had had a hell of a time with her – 'Please sir can I have some more', routine.

Today I had a new challenge. Betty (one of my wards) had witnessed the patient opposite her two nights previous on a different ward suffer a fatal cardiac arrest and was understandably very anxious. I totally got that it was hard when you had a demanding patient, we all had had our fair share, but some staff just weren't cut out for them, and I didn't ever appreciate a handover that focussed on the opinions of personal dramatics of a patient. I took it on the chin and carried on with my morning safety checks. As I approached Betty's bed, she was sleeping comfortably with her CPAP mask on and even though I was as quiet as a mouse she still managed to hear me and open her eyes.

"Morning," I had greeted her quietly with a smile.

"Stay with me," she immediately responded. *For the love of God*, I thought.

"Of course, I need to do your morning medications anyway," is what actually travelled out of my mouth.

Betty was a young lady in her late thirties with mousey blonde hair and an overgrown fringe, very greasy and overdue a wash, but that was the 'norm' for patients on our unit as they were confined to their bed space and there were too many electricals and the head straps for the masks/nasal cannulas left no room for a quick hair wash.

"They want to take me this off," she said, pointing to her mask, I already knew this though because my task for the day was to coax her off the mask and onto a normal 'venturi mask' – what is used as standard practice for patients needing a normal supply of oxygen. It made a difference having to persuade someone to ditch the high-flow oxygen therapy, I had spent the last four months forcing it onto people!

The doctors did their round and were less than impressed that Betty was still taking up a bed, using high-flow oxygen and is refusing to step down so I re-assured them that we would have it in hand by the afternoon round. I had a knack of promising the impossible and managing to deliver and today had been no different.

I had started with the hair. I managed to convince Betty that if she were to go on the normal mask for a break, I would wheel her to the bathroom and give her hair a lovely wash. Apprehensive at first, she finally agreed. Unfortunately, as soon as I removed the CPAP mask, she had a panic attack, claiming she couldn't breathe and was suffocating, quite convincingly too, as I recall. With the mask firmly back on, we discussed what had just happened, she told a very graphic story of how the person opposite her had suffered a cardiac arrest and how she had heard one of the nurses saying, 'If only they had worn the bloody mask'. Now we were all guilty of saying this as the majority of time it was true, people who refused to wear the mask as prescribed tended to deteriorate a lot quicker than those who complied; however, a cardiac arrest wouldn't be the direct result of not wearing a mask.

An hour later and I had explained every scenario I had encountered, told tales of the many people who I had to coax to wear the mask, those who did well and those who didn't, honesty was the best policy in my mind. She agreed to take the mask off and try the high-flow nasal, I wasn't hopeful but after a while she came too and was tolerating it immensely which was primarily due to it being on the lowest setting as she didn't require a huge amount of oxygen. This was life changing for Betty as she had been eating and drinking very little of late in fear of the mask being off for more than a few seconds at a time. I was halfway there now; eating, drinking, and being able to hold a conversation with her partner over FaceTime, she appeared a lot happier and relaxed, I thought I would give it a few hours before we took the next step down.

4 p.m. and the afternoon rounds had begun. I approached Betty.

"Let's show the doctors how far you have come, eh?" I encouraged her. Although clearly apprehensive she agreed.

"As long as you hold my hand." I love a good hand holding so was happy to oblige. I started by putting the venturi-mask over her nasal cannula and once happy we removed the nasal and then she was sitting comfortably on 15 litres venturi mask, no more high-flow oxygen therapy for this lady – she was exceeding her oxygen saturations. I was like a prized pony when the doctors approached, astounded and delighted as they were, they were desperate to push it one step too far.

"Let's step down to a ward," they announced. Panic immediately struck and Betty began to have an attack, luckily I was able to calm her and re-assure her whilst giving the doctors a Sarah-glare.

"Let's see how we get on tonight," I stropped, "and we can review in the morning." Now this is one of the things I loved about working on CPAP, doctors listened to us nurses suddenly, we were the guru's and our voices mattered, they agreed and moved on. Sarah 1 - Doctors 0.

As challenging a day as it was, I had succeeded. Betty was

on her way to getting better, I had won my challenge with the doctors, the night staff were overly impressed, and I was ready for home, as tomorrow I switched back onto nights yay!

*

Just one random night shift scheduled, they were the worst as you couldn't get into a pattern, they really screwed with your body clock. The joy! I was back with Glynis who was still on hourly blood sugar monitoring, a CPAP mask, and in need of feeding. Handover finished and Glynis was not happy about seeing me at all.

"You're going to starve me," she sighed on my arrival at her bedside. She said it as though it was my life ambition to ensure that she didn't get fed, despite my re-assurance that I wouldn't starve her, but I would not be allowing any midnight snacking.

"I hate you!" she responded. I felt as though I was babysitting a spoilt teenager rather than someone in their thirties. *Is that all you've got?* I thought to myself as I left her to sulk. Evening medications completed and I had Glynis and another lady who wasn't showing any signs of improvement and was in the queue for the dreaded side room, a very frail, old lady who was peacefully sleeping, not a pick of bother at all.

It was 10 p.m. that night and Glynis requested a cup of tea and biscuit, I agreed and served up what I hoped would be the final request for food of the evening. All was quiet and off I trotted on break, it was just after 2 a.m. the next morning when I returned and there was Glynis chomping away at cheese and crackers, one of the few staple foods to be found in the fridge. She gave me a big smile, toasting me with her cheese and crackers as I entered the nurse's station.

"Sorry, she was crying, there was nothing I could do," said my colleague who was covering my section whilst I was on break. "Her blood sugar was okay for her," she continued as she tried to justify her actions. Everyone is an individual and what was high for Glynis was probably life threatening for others. I was not a happy bunny. Once finished, I visited Glynis quickly, popping her mask on.

"Just two jobs today, breathe and sleep," I told her.

All was quiet for about an hour, that was until Glynis started with the tears.

"I'm starving!" In my head, I was thinking, *This bloody woman wouldn't know starving if it hit her face on.*

"Come on now, Glynis," I had encouraged her, "you can NOT be hungry, it's time for sleep—"

"Please, just a biscuit!" she sobbed. I stood firm but I sat with her until she finally cried herself to sleep, as heartless as it sounded, she needed rest more than food.

6 a.m. and Glynis had been asleep for almost three hours; she hadn't even stirred for her hourly finger pricks. I forego her 6 a.m. medications as they were not time precious and could be given at 8 a.m. with breakfast. The day staff arrived and were dumbfounded that I had managed to curb the eating and that Glynis was asleep. I must be honest, I had pinched her a few times just to check she was breathing. As I left the unit, I gave her one last check, she was doing great, little could be said for my other patient as the side room had been vacated in the early hours of the morning and she was

ready to be transported there by the day staff. As I said my goodbyes, I was really sad once again, it was never nice moving someone to the side room but luckily she was completely oblivious as to what was to come.

As I returned to my day shifts, Glynis had been stepped down to a normal ward, she was off her hourly observations and on her way to getting better. I had pinned her down initially to be one of the victims of Covid, how wrong was I, she superseded all our expectations. Good on her, things were beginning to change.

CHAPTER 13

TIMES, THEY ARE A CHANGING

It was creeping towards the end of February 2021, I was a year older having celebrated a birthday and we were starting to see the change in patients we were treating, most of whom were on the road to recovery and the high-flow oxygen therapy was a nice-to-have opposed to a must-have.

It was a Wednesday night shift and the back unit had one patient, I'd been assigned to look after him for the evening. He wasn't a Covid patient, he was in fact a cardiology patient and being the only trained Cardiology nurse on the unit it was a no brainer. Now when I say 'trained' I mean it loosely as I had only been on the unit as a newly qualified nurse a matter of weeks before we had been transformed into a makeshift high dependency respiratory unit, even so I knew more than the others. Philip was a very poorly gentleman, he was mid-fifties, stocky in build with a beer gut to be proud of, he was desperate to watch the football in peace so we agreed that he could watch the football if he promised to behave for the evening. By behave I meant no cardiac arrests. He had been placed in our care for the evening as he was due to be taken to our sister hospital first thing in the morning for a triple heart bypass, he was literally a ticking time bomb!

It was very eerie and lonely where we were, I kept to my promise and did not disturb Philip whilst he watched the match, he was in a proper sulk as his team lost and wanted to sleep. His request for me to not disturb him throughout the evening was duly noted, he was hooked up to a machine anyway so there was no need to interrupt his sleep. Oh my goodness there was no need for his machine either, he snored like a warthog! He even made me sleepy with his constant rhythmic snoring. It was 1 a.m. and I decided to keep myself awake by doing some of my patient write ups, a bit early but the constant snoring had my eyes struggling to stay open.

Happily typing away at the nurse's station, I felt a sudden yank on the back of chair, it was so forceful that I had immediately swung round, angry face at the ready expecting to see one of the other nurses or healthcares there. No one was there and I could feel the hairs stand up all over my body. I am not one for believing in all things supernatural, but I tell you now it was the most frightening thing ever. I slowly moved away from the nurse's station and positioned my chair with the back against the wall because a) no one would be able to sneak up behind me, b) I could see everyone in front of me and c) there was no way I was going through that again.

It was 3.30 a.m. and the healthcare came to relieve me for my break, I had never been so relieved to see anyone in my entire life.

"Why are you sat like that?" she laughed, I didn't want to tell her in case she didn't want to cover my break, so I sheepishly lied.

"Oh, I'm just stretching my legs out." Luckily, she bought it and off I 'ran' on my break. Throughout the Covid pandemic I never really took my full break allocation on nights, but that night I damn well made sure I did. I returned to the ward and decided to come clean with the healthcare, she was not impressed at all, she was (as it turned out) very superstitious, which I already knew as she would never go near patients who had passed on her own.

It was 6 a.m. and time to wake Philip up early, he was first on the list and his transport was booked for 7 a.m. As I stood over him sleeping (creepy I know), I couldn't help but feel grateful as he had been very well behaved – no dramas, no demands, the perfect patient. I gave him a good shake, explained how he had snored the entire evening and replaced the need for all the heart monitors on him, he chuckled.

"My wife says I am the worst snorer in London."

"I think she meant the world, Phillip!" I replied and we laughed, having to have bland food only he agreed to a bowl of porridge and water, a true 'Oliver Twist' breakfast this was. He wanted to have a shower which I totally got as goodness knows when he would be able to have one after his operation. I agreed to remove his wire if he sat whilst he showered and the door could be left open, the last thing I wanted was for any drama now. He did not disappoint; he was the perfect patient despite telling the transport people I was a 'Peeping Tom'. He was off on his way to have his operation, that night was as good as it got despite my uninvited guest.

*

The following evening and I was back for another night shift, the rear unit was still empty, and we had only six patients at the front with only two requiring oxygen therapies, seventy percent of wards had now reverted to their previous non-Covid status, and it looked as though the hospital was through the storm.

My patient for the evening was a lady name Shania, she had given birth to her daughter three weeks prior in the hospital, she had been intubated in intensive care and had been stepped down to us a few hours prior. These patients always broke my heart, imagine giving birth and not being able to see or touch your child. It was her first child, and she was doing amazing. She only required minimal oxygen therapy through the high-flow nasal cannula and I was determined to have her weaned off it so she could go to a normal ward where hopefully, as it was no longer a Covid area, she could have her daughter visit.

As I approached Shania's bed she was sleeping, as I gently woke her, she appeared so happy to see me. Her hair was jet black slicked back afro, her dark piercing eyes full of happiness.

"Hi," she beamed.

"Hello," I replied equally as happily. "I'm Sarah, your nurse, I'm just here to do your evening medications."

"Okay," she replied, still beaming, and sat herself up in bed, she radiated happiness and I warmed to her immediately. Evening medications administered, we agreed to try her on the normal venturi mask, after all she was doing great on the lowest settings of high flow, this was a bit of a risk as patients needing high flow tended to be more reliant during the evenings, but I was determined to give it a shot even if it meant I had to stay at her bedside all evening. She was in full agreement, I promised to stay at her bedside, and she promised to breathe. It was as easy as that. This is the most heart breaking, yet most caring initiative of the maternity unit, they had taken videos of her daughter twice, sometimes three times a day for her whilst she was intubated, documenting her progress to ensure that Shania didn't miss out. *Oh, my goodness!* Only 4lb born at 32 weeks she was tiny, yet had a full head of black hair, I watched all the videos and it was an amazing experience to see her day by day get stronger, no longer requiring her feeding tubes she was almost ready to go home. Having only met Shania that evening, I was in love, she was going to make an amazing mum to her daughter, I could just tell. It didn't faze her that she had missed out on the first 23 days of her life, she took that in her stride and appreciated the rest of the life they had to look forward to together.

I kept my promise (apart from a couple of brief comfort breaks) and stayed at Shania's bedside throughout the evening making positional changes as opposed to re-applying the oxygen therapy and she had a successful night without the need for high-flow oxygen therapy intervention. The Night Doctor did a quick round so he could handover to the Day Doctors, and he was confident that Shania could be moved off the unit to a normal ward where she would finally be able to get to meet her daughter in real life. I was elated, we were both elated, this was a feeling I had not been accustomed to in over four months, since the day I wheeled Frances up to the main entrance if I was being honest. This was hopefully the start of a new chapter of nothing but happy stories.

Saturday morning, I had a blessed two days off with the

family and would be back on shift first thing Monday morning. I greeted my husband and his trusty canine steed that morning with a smile, for once I could offload a happy story, he appeared just as elated as I did.

We were finally winning!

*

It was Monday morning, the first week in March 2021, it was a lovely crisp morning, mild for the time of year I thought. I was ready for the day ahead.

As I entered the unit it had been transformed! There were no warning signs for entering a Covid unit, there was no donning on station for PPE. I entered the staff room and a familiar colleague sat in her nurse's uniform, it was one of the ward nurses who had elected not to stay with the ward when it had transitioned to a high dependency Covid Unit and now she was back.

"Miss me?" she asked.

"Of course! But what's happening?" The unit had been vacated by Covid patients late on the Saturday and had gone under a deep clean and fogging throughout Sunday.

"And we're returning to normal today?" I asked. I was then subjected to a brief run-down of her story, quickly coming to the realisation that this nurse was clearly deluded and had no idea what we had been through as a team the previous four plus months as all she did was whine and moan about how hard it had been working in an unfamiliar ward. I just let her witter on, so did Sandy, a fellow nurse who, like me, had elected to stay on the unit throughout the second wave. I think it's fair to say we were both shell shocked at how quick things had been turned around. There were no patients on the unit at this point, there was no handover to be had and we were just to plan for the day. We were to receive all urgent Cardiology patients who had been scattered throughout the hospital in the weeks prior, all deemed to be in serious condition as they had not been in the specialist care area they needed.

It sounded like a good plan but what happened over the next few weeks was an abomination.

We had requested time to debrief and recover before we went back to full capacity (26 beds), but that obviously fell on deaf ears as before it was even lunch time we were almost full. It was as if an announcement had gone out across the three sites, 'Attention all staff. All the weird, wonderful, patients including those with unexplainable ailments are to be sent to Sarah's Ward straight away, I repeat ... all weird, wonderful, ever so slightly odd patients including those with the oddest of ailments to be sent to Sarah's Ward ASAP'. I generally was not one to whine or shirk responsibilities, but I must admit I was struggling, I had gone from 1-4 appreciative patients to 6-8 demanding, mostly ungrateful patients.

*

Shift three of returning to 'normal' and I was even more exhausted. I had entered the unit to the unmistakable smell of urine, and I mean it stunk. We had a patient who was found unconscious in the street, intoxicated with whatever, suffering from heart failure and fluid overload. Patients suffering from heart failure and fluid overload required an intravenous drug named furosemide, the purpose of which was to remove excess fluid from the body mainly through urination. Patients who received this treatment usually had a urinary catheter in place for their comfort but not this patient, to be named Gordon. Gordon simply did not want a catheter, refused to use a bottle and thought it appropriate to just piss everywhere in protest of not being able to walk to the toilet. Why wasn't he allowed to walk to the toilet? you ask, well the simple answer to that was he couldn't. His legs were weeping, requiring dressings from his toes to his knees, they were so swollen due to the fluid retention that they'd split, no shoes or non-slip socks fitted, meaning it was unsafe for him to walk on the ward's floors.

Gordon had been on the unit less than 24 hours, and he had caused so much trouble, patients were arguing with him constantly due to his demands and attitudes towards the staff and despite the efforts to clean up after him the place smelt like a urinal in a pub that hadn't been cleaned in weeks. Gordon was placed in bed five, a privileged bed next to a window, a bed most would die for as family were able to stand outside and talk to the patients, but Gordon had no family and due to his antics, his partner had thrown him out three weeks prior, leaving him to be homeless. Ten minutes at Gordon's bedside and it became quickly apparent why she'd thrown him out. The healthcare was trying to get Gordon changed after he had decided to urinate in his chair before breakfast. I am removed from the drama at this point, sorting his morning medications out, but I was fully aware of his behaviour.

I made my presence known.

"Morning Gordon!" I exclaimed cheery and smiling as ever.

"Where the fuck you from? Scotland?" was the gruff response.

"No, Newcastle," I responded assertively.

"Might as well be Scotland," he scoffed.

"Actually, not at all, now stop the attitude and take your meds," I had responded calmly. I could see by the grimace on his face he was not impressed at all, but I was giving him no more attitude than he had with the Healthcare Assistants as they washed him down.

I had moved swiftly on to my next patient (I had eight patients in my care today), to be greeted with a relieved smile.

"Thank god you're here today, you won't take much shit off him, will you?" I winked and explained it was not about taking the shit, it was about making sure he had the best care needed to get him well enough to be shipped elsewhere. Simon was his name, he was in his late twenties, needing treatment for a DVT (deep vein thrombosis – blood clot in the leg), there had been a lot of speculation in the news that this was linked as a side effect to the Oxford/AstraZeneca vaccine and little more than four weeks later it was announced as a confirmed link, being fatal if left untreated. Luckily for Simon his sister-in-law was a nurse and had recognised the signs of a DVT, prompting him to seek treatment.

Back to Gordon, it wasn't even 11 a.m. and he had been changed several times, now sitting on a towel he was just happily sat there dribbling away. *Give me strength!* I thought as I approached his bed.

"Change my dressings," he demanded. *What was the point, they we getting wet from all the pissing?* I had spoken to the Tissue Viability Team who refused to review unless he had a catheter in place as the dressing were ineffective, he was to continue urinating through them. I felt like I was fighting a losing battle. Gordon refused a catheter, continued to urinate everywhere, demanding that people clean up after him, he was pushing buttons on all levels. The doctors continued to increase his furosemide, wanting him on a continuous drip 24 hours a day. I challenged the doctors, there was no way I was putting him on a continuous intravenous drip unless he had a catheter in, his legs were becoming infected, the unit stunk of urine, it was an unfair request. I lost the battle because without the continuous administration of furosemide he would most probably die, I needed to find a middle ground with Gordon and his right of pissing everywhere.

It was 6 p.m., I had still not changed Gordon's leg dressings and I was about to attach him to the continuous administration of furosemide. He was what I could only describe as 'vile'. Harsh as I know that sounds, there was simply no other to refer to him.

"It's your job to clean up my piss!" "Change my dressings!" Blahdy blah! I was beyond exhausted and sick of this man's entitlement.

"Is it also our job to receive non-stop abuse and demands from you?" I asked.

"You get paid to do as I say, clean me up now!" he demanded. This was by far the most challenging patient I had dealt with as a qualified nurse, but I would not be defeated, I threw him a towel and a clean pair of pyjama bottoms.

"There's nothing wrong with your hands, clean yourself up and let me know when you're done and I will help with the pulling of your bottoms up." He was lost for words, but he did as I instructed. He removed his wet bottoms, dried himself down, and once finished I helped pull his bottoms over his feet. I warned him that the drip would create a continuous drip of urine and a catheter would be the best course of action, it would also have the benefits of tissue viability reviewing him in the hope of getting better dressings in his legs, with the aim of getting him mobilising again.

"Yeah, fuck off home I'm fine as I am!"

And with that I said a cheery "Goodnight then." *You can't save them all*, I told myself, straight home and a long shower, I felt like I stunk of piss despite my husband's assurances to the contrary.

CHAPTER 14

YOU COULDN'T WRITE IT

It was mid-March and although we had only been a few weeks back as a Cardiology ward, the stress was palpable, feelings of exhaustion more so than ever, there had still been no de-briefing of the previous months and we were drowning in patients.

Day one of three long days, I was at the rear end of the unit again which had now been turned into lady's bay, this was a nine-bed unit with two nurses covering, no Healthcare but it meant the maximum patients per nurse was limited to five opposed to eight at the front. I was having a proper feel-sorry-for-myself day, barely spoke a word since I had got up (very rare), but that was all about to change. As I entered the unit there was a buzz in the air, the nurse on charge came bouncing down the corridor.

"You're never going to believe it!" She was right, I didn't believe it, but I remembered Xenia, the lady who has suffered a cardiac arrest while screaming at her husband, one minute she was giving it what-for on her phone the next she was flat lined. There she was sat up right in her bed, her dark hair still as wild as ever, her dark piercing eyes fixated on her iPad. I was like a giddy child grinning from ear to ear as I approached her.

"Remember me?" Of course she didn't, she thankfully had no recollection of any of the events surrounding our previous meeting, which for her was good. She was to be one of my patients for the day, I was elated. Xenia had spent the previous six weeks in our sister hospital on ECMO initially, then intubated and back to us once stable to have an ICD (defibrillator) fitted.

Xenia had been through so much; it was believed her cardiac arrest was triggered by hypoglycaemia – low blood sugar levels.

'Hypoglycaemia-induced sudden cardiac death results from enhanced adrenergic signalling at the level of the heart that leads to sinus tachycardia. Tachycardia is followed by third-degree heart block that culminates into a fatal bradycardic rhythm causing cardiorespiratory failure and sudden death.'

Although this was the belief of their findings it was not conclusive, blood sugar levels can be monitored and controlled, one in eleven people live with diabetes and have the arduous task of monitoring their blood-sugar levels. Xenia's arrest came from nowhere and the decision to have an ICD was not taken lightly, especially not by her.

I had spent the day with Xenia, she was so grateful for everything we had done and continued to do; she did, however, resent the fact that this had happened to her.

"I feel like an old lady," she said repeatedly and despite my re-assurance it was what it was, I could tell she was in a world of limbo, she should be thankful for surviving, yet pitiful for the life-changing impact it will have on her.

Xenia was placed next to the nurse's station which stood right in the middle of the bay area, opposite Xenia was a frail old lady named Dot. Now Dot was one of those challenging patients we hated to love, she was a dementia patient who had collapsed at home, which she shared with her daughter and son-in-law.

Dot was fully clothed with her cream trousers and brown jumper with a white t-shirt poking out the top, she had silver hair, cut perfectly to her shoulders, she looked her tender age of seventy-nine. She just sat there without making a sound, watching the goings on around her.

It was my first contact with Dot which was going to determine the rest of my day, she hadn't said a word as I measured out all her tablets into her pot, she had just watched patiently.

"Are you able to take these all at once?" I asked.

"What a stupid question," she responded, I had barely taken my hand from the cup of tablets and whoosh she had downed them.

"You'd be great on a night out in Newcastle," I joked.

"Why? Do I look like a slapper?" she responded. Had I been drinking my cuppa I would have sprayed it in her face with laughter.

I could hear the peals of laughter from the nurse and the

patient beds around me. I tried to justify my comments, rapidly explaining how in Newcastle we like to have shots, but she didn't buy it and proceeded to talk about Newcastle girls being 'slappers' and 'right goers'. I had left her to it by this point, she was in full swing of conversation with Xenia about how she had known a Geordie lass who had liked to put it about. I didn't take offense at all, it was quite funny and worked wonders to cheer everyone up, even at my expense it was more than welcomed.

Breakfast and washes were almost done, there was no need for Dot to have a wash as she had been up with the larks and the night staff had seen to her, but she did need a cannula in for a scan. One of the young doctors asked to do it as he needed the practice, I warned him that she was a feisty one and had, from what I had seen, very poor vein access. He had just laughed at me, I couldn't blame him, she looked like a sweet old lady, like butter wouldn't have melted in her mouth. I had insisted on assisting him as the night staff had disclosed that all though old and sweet, she had been quite threatening with her fists, unbelievable as it was, she was barely 'two stone wet' as my dad would say.

There she sat with a big smile on her face, Doctor Nigel greeted her back with an even bigger one.

"Morning Dot, how are you today?"

"Well I was fine till *she* called me a slapper this morning," she responded, flicking a gesture at me. *For the love of God how did she even remember our earlier conversation?* The doctor just looked at me with a big smirk, despite my protest I just went along with him, what a tale she spun him. Fifteen minutes later and he was still no further forward, he had done the worst thing ever and engaged into what turned out a lengthy conversation with Dot. I had decided at this point she was not deluded at all, she was in fact as crafty as they come. She was stalling him.

Doctor Nigel finally got consent from Dot, whilst he was preparing his bits, she raised her tiny fist to me like my Grandad used to do to my little brother when he misbehaved.

"I'll give him this right on the end of his nose if he hurts me!" she exclaimed. Now this didn't surprise me, but did take Dr Nigel by surprise, he had looked terrified.

"No need for that, Dot," he had wearyingly responded. I had placed myself on the edge of Dot's bed so I could ensure that the fist waving could be easily controlled by the gentle placing on my hand.

"You better change that blanket after your bits have been on them!" she quipped. *What the actual ...!?* was running through my mind. I used the insult to my advantage, distracting her whilst gently holding her little fist hand down.

"Tell me where my bits had been?" I had responded as innocently as I possibly can, feigning being hurt. It didn't work, she had been fixated on Dr Nigel, her free hand firmly placed between mine, Dr Nigel held the other as he attempted to place the cannula in her hand.

"You dirty robbing bastard!" she screamed, I had assured her there was no need for that as Dr Nigel was just doing his job.

"He's a charlatan!" she shouted. "Get him off me!" Dr Nigel glanced nervously at me, I nodded for him to continue, to which he did and eventually.

"All done!" he announced as he quickly stood up before leaving go of her hand. As I had stood up, her fist came from nowhere.

"Come here, let me give it to you!" Although she had looked angry and convincingly intent on using it, she was no threat as I was soon to find out.

It was after lunch and the call for Dot to go and have her scan had been received, I needed to get her into a gown, which sounded a lot easier than it was. Dot could keep her bottoms on, but I needed to remove her top half and get her into bed. Dot was unsteadying on her feet, she could muster a shuffled walk holding onto you so to kill two birds with one stone we shuffled together like in a conga to the bathroom. As we entered the bathroom the fist was already waving.

"If you hurt me, you will get this," she promised. Xenia and the other patients chuckled as I had manoeuvred her past their beds, giving them a gentle smile to re-assure them that she was in fact harmless.

Dot was perched on the toilet having finished her wee. I began to remove her tops, all whilst doing so she had the most mischievous look, fist still clenched. She meant business.

"Put that down," I had joked with her, "you'll put your eye out with it." She happily kept it there, sniggering away to herself. We had shuffled back to the bed, everyone was pleased to see I hadn't been beaten to a pulp by Dot. The Student Nurse who was assisting us asked if she could watch the scan. Who was I to stand in the way of learning? It saved me a trip, so I had agreed.

It was 4 p.m. and Dot had returned from her scan. I was at Xenia's bedside, we were looking at what she could watch later that evening as the Student Nurse scurried over, the look of horror on her face.

"That was so embarrassing," she said and as I had guided her from earshot of Xenia.

"Tell me more," I had encouraged. Apparently, the fist had made an almost immediate appearance, Dot had insulted the entire team by calling them 'incompetent idiots' and was 'going to see them all outside' and was intending to 'beat them to a pulp one by one'. I couldn't help but laugh, as when we had looked over there she sat upright in her bed, a matchstick frail old lady eating a biscuit, giving all a gentle cheery wave as they passed.

Dot was harmless, I had wondered what she had been like when she was younger. I had visions of her being like Pat Butcher from *EastEnders*, she had that aura about her. Xenia had been scheduled for her operation the following day, she had been having second thoughts, but the Junior Sister and I had re-assured her it was for the best. Xenia trusted our judgement and prepared herself for the following morning.

There he was, waiting with his canine partner in crime, the husband found the stories of the day's events hilarious, so did the parents when I FaceTimed them later that evening. We were all loving the fact that Xenia had made it back to us.

The morning came quick enough, I was at the rear again with the women, Xenia's operation had been put back to the following day due to staff shortages, it was devastating as this was her final hurdle to overcome before she could go home.

Given that she had been a true success story we decided that we would arrange a collection, get her some flowers, and do a guard of honour out of the unit, symbolising her courage. Dot's scans had shown no coronary issues and it was put down to an accidental fall, so she was to be discharged that evening. It was about now that the comment about Dot being Pat Butcher from *EastEnders* was to become a reality. I'd had a day of fist waving, threats, and name calling from her but all in good fun, I think she just loved the attention. As I had wheeled Dot through to the main entrance, there stood a stocky lady with short, cropped blonde hair nad leopard print woolly coat on, It was Pat minus the earrings.

"'Ope you been behavin!" she shouted at us with a thick London accent. I wasn't sure if she was talking to me or Dot! Never one to tell tales, I laughed and handed Dot over. I was actually going to miss her, abuse and all. Back on the ward I said my final good nights, another day done and off home I went.

The following morning, I was allocated at the front with the males, the males were less demanding than females, two days of constant commodes was enough to tip anyone over the edge and at least with the males it was mostly a wee bottle needed. Handover had finished, I had rushed to the back to wish Xenia luck, but I had missed her by seconds. Should I or shouldn't I nip round to theatres (this was part of the unit on the opposite side)? I told myself, *no you have eight men waiting for their morning medications, Sarah, you will see her soon enough.*

Little less than an hour later I was in the female bay when Xenia was wheeled in.

"Wow that was quick!" I said, frowned, and glanced at the

Junior Sister who had obviously had the same thought. There were only two theatre staff, they had a full list and thought it better to wheel Xenia straight out of theatre back onto the unit. They had thought wrong, I took one look at Xenia and I knew there was something up, she had been mumbling to me, she had been happy to see me. Duly noted that her last set of observations were low, I immediately questioned them but the theatre nurses flippantly re-assured me that it was due to the mild sedative given in theatre, fifteen-minute clinical observations and rest they demanded. I had needed to get back to my males, so I said my goodbyes to Xenia, told the Junior Sister to call if she needed anything, promising to pop round as much as I could spare.

I was barely at the entrance to the male bay when the emergency buzzer sounded, I knew who it was – I had the most dreadful sinking feeling in the pit of my stomach. The crash trolley was kept in the male bay area, I had gone into auto mode, unplugged the trolley and running with it to the female bay, it was a repeat of the first time, but this time there were more of us. The trainee associate was putting the call out, one nurse was doing compressions, whilst the other was holding the oxygen mask securely in place. It was different from the first time, it had been first thing in the morning and the Doctors were already there, there were more hands on deck. I had taken a step back, there were more than enough 'cooks in the kitchen' and I stood in shock which seemed like forever but had been merely minutes. Xenia had an ICD in place, so she had already been receiving shocks in her heart, so she had been semi-conscious when the compressions had been started and had become very afraid.

I had returned to the male bay when the trainee nursing associate came for me, they couldn't calm Xenia down, she had been screaming out for me. They had needed to get her to sit still for a chest x-ray but couldn't. As soon as she saw me, she calmed down.

"I'm not going anywhere, Xenia, it's alright," I re-assured her, "we're in this together, remember? We've come too far for it to end now." This was the first time I had no gloves or visor on whilst comforting a patient post Covid, I still had a mask on, it felt how nursing had been when I had started my training, it felt humane.

The x-ray had showed a bleed, with no theatres available as the surgeon who had performed the operation was now mid-surgery elsewhere. He did, however, make an appearance advising that he had thought he had 'nicked an artery', a very rare occurrence in such a simple procedure.

"There had been no signs of bleeding post procedure," the theatre staff and surgeon had protested. Truth of the matter was that she should have been monitored in the recovery bay, staff or not no-one else should have been taken into that theatre until it was established that Xenia was stable, an investigation would follow, rest assured it was, but we were not made aware of its findings.

The x-ray had showed the left side of lung almost rubbed out in darkness, that was the bleed, she was slowly drowning. She had received two pints of blood before stabilising enough to be transferred to theatre at our sister hospital. I had kept my promise and stayed with her until she was ready to leave. We had joked how Prince Philip had stayed at the hospital and had received care at the hand of the unit she was going to, Princess Xenia like the TV show *Warrior Princess* I had watched when I was younger. It was hard to say goodbye to Xenia, she had come so far. *Please let this end well for her.*

The following day, although off shift, my ward manager messaged me Xenia had gone in for surgery, the 'nip' had closed itself and the excess blood was happily being absorbed back into her body, she was going to survive!

Ten days later she was finally discharged home. I never got to see her again, maybe one day our paths would cross again, she was either the luckiest or unluckiest person I knew.

CHAPTER 15

TIME FOR A CHANGE

As a family we had decided we wanted to relocate back to Newcastle at the start of May 2021. My husband was now a permanent home worker, my son was graduating his NFL course and my daughter would continue her degree in London. I felt I was at the point of no return, I was unashamedly exhausted both physically and emotionally, it was time to be with family. I had secured a job as a nurse in the Occupational Health team. As much as I was looking forward to it, I was riddled with guilt, I was leaving my new-found family in London who had come to rely on me. Before I was to leave the dramas were far from done and there were a few more tales to tell about finishing my time in the nation's capital.

Night shifts were soon to be a thing of the past to me, and I was on a roll for my last three. Night shifts were highly sought after by some of the staff (a quieter shift, a higher shift allowance, no social life etc.), but at the peak of the second wave there simply weren't the staff to afford the luxury of being choosey. It was an unusual night, nice and crisp for mid-April, a good night for walking, I just had to survive these three nights then two weeks of days and I would be done.

There, stood outside the side room, were two security guards, one a young man with jet black hair and dark complexion, and the other in his mid-forties, olive skin with a bald head. Unlike the security in Newcastle these guys looked the business; stab vests, handcuffs, pepper spray, you name it they had the lot and sat beside them was a plump middle-aged lady, in some tunic and trousers but not a nurse and not of the trust either.

"Evening," I greeted them all, to be met with a stony silence. I shrugged my shoulders and toddled off to the nurse's station. I expressed my happiness to my colleagues and dismay at our guests to which they were not surprised, they had had a hell of a day. With nowhere to put the gentleman currently in the side room for his safety, he had been given to us to 'babysit', I say babysit light-heartedly as that's what we ended up doing.

The man, named Tyson, was in his late fifties, he had been found unconscious in the street, he had two black eyes, stitches across his forehead and the left side of his cheek, he had most certainly been in the wars. With no recollection of events, obvious aggression and confusion, he was assigned to us. Why not, we had been non-Covid now for almost five weeks and we had been given all the weird, wonderful, and special souls who needed a home.

I began my evening medications round and decided to leave the ominous side room until last. Everyone was in for fluid offloading or awaiting some sort of cardiology procedure, it was the male bay so except for one patient they were mostly independent, so not a bad mix. Mid-way through my round there were screams of commotion from the side room, I stopped what I was doing to investigate. I was perplexed; the patient had managed to pull the pane of glass out from its frame and escaped, the smaller of the two-security guard stood in shock.

"What shall I do?" he exclaimed.

Calmly and assertively I responded, "Get your arse through that window and bring him back!"

The look on his face was priceless but give him his dues he went through the window and gave chase. The older security guard had already fled out of the unit, he was obviously fearful that I was going to demand his scrawny arse get through the window as well. Within minutes, they had returned, one security guard either side of a highly amused Tyson dragging him back through, laughing and joking as they placed him back in the room. Until the window could be fixed, one of the guards had to sit in with him.

I had continued my medications round, despite the dramas no-one was going anywhere anytime soon. It had been time to tackle Tyson. He was an alcoholic, he needed intravenous intervention which he had refused and had already removed three cannulas throughout the day. His room had been stripped bare, he had taken the covers off the bed and pillows, refused to have any equipment in the room, it looked like a prison sell, a bed frame, blue plastic mattress, with two blue plastic pillows. He was sat there in the chair closest to the door as security guarded the window on the far side of the room. I remember thinking, *What a bloody mess*. Tyson was slouched in this chair, eyes barely opened due to the swelling and bruising of his black eyes, dried blood on his face, hands and clothes, most likely from the self-removal of cannulas throughout the day.

"Fuck off," were his first slurred words to me. *Time for some Geordie charm,* I thought,

"Any need for that sort of welcome?" At the sound of my Geordie accident, he immediately snapped to attention. I had been astonished; I would normally get 'You from Scotland?' (Even had a "Fuck off!" back thereto), or Ireland or Wales but he knew where I was from immediately.

"Right, no more dramas tonight, I'm not up for it, so you needed to stop here and now." He laughed.

"What's in it for me?"

"The difference between happy Geordie fish wife and a grumpy one." Now this made him smile, I hoped he wasn't all bad and his behaviour was that of alcohol withdrawal. On a previous ward, he had managed to crack a nurse's rib when she had attempted to give him his medications, but I was not to hold that against him, but I did apply more caution on approach. Initially he had refused his medications, including his pain relief, so I let him be.

"I've got some pain relief for you, give me a shout if you want them." I wouldn't be far from his room, two security guards and a registered mental health nurse outside his room and he still managed to escape, that would be investigated over the coming days.

It was 11 p.m., the ward was quiet, patients were beginning to settle for the evening when the older security guard approached. Tyson had asked to see me. He wanted his pain relief and I managed to get him to take all his medications, bribery some would say, gentle persuasion others. He had been exhausted and awake for almost thirty-six hours so the pain relief would have a drowsy effect on him. Also, I had coaxed him onto the bed with the promise I would be there when he woke up, he had still refused any blankets and was now curled in the foetal position with just his blood-stained jeans and navy-blue polo shirt, he must have been freezing. Once he was almost unconscious, I placed bedding over him. He didn't make a sound, just snuggled up in it.

I had a shorter break that evening, just in case Tyson awoke and started causing havoc, but he didn't. I even prodded him a few times just to check he was still breathing. The registered mental health nurse had spent most of the evening either talking to the security guard or sleeping herself and I began to question what her role was. 6 a.m. medications were done and dusted, everyone was so appreciative of my efforts of the peaceful evening and were delighted to my dismay that I was back that evening for round two. I had popped my head in on Tyson on my way past and he was in the same position he had been all night, so I headed off home.

I returned that evening, the same two security guards and the mental health nurse stood guard outside the side room, this time they had responded when I had said evening.

A very different day had been had. Although still very confused, the thirteen-hour sleep that he had endured had been very effective – the day staff allowed him to wake naturally – what they meant was they had let sleeping dogs lie. The previous night I had left Tyson until last on my round and to my disappointment and anger he was still wearing the same blood-stained jeans and polo shirt. When I announced my presence in his room, he had looked confused.

"Let me guess," I said, "you know the voice, but you don't know where from?" I was right, he had no recollection of the previous day's events, despite everyone reliving them for him he was oblivious, except for having spoken to a Geordie lass. I had noticed a holdall in the corner of the room, retrieving clean tracksuit bottoms and T-shirt I made him change. He needed guidance because above all else he was still a withdrawing alcoholic, confused and vulnerable. He had refused his medications all day, I hadn't held up much hope for the evening ones, but he took them without any resistance. He had claimed that no-one had offered him any, but I took that with a pinch of salt. He had allowed me to check and clean his wounds on his face and they were brutal, he would have some nasty scares. Tyson told me he was jumped by a group of lads for his watch, maybe it was true, maybe it wasn't?

He slept on and off in his chair throughout the night, I think the mental health nurse got more sleep than him, not one to tell tales, I did however report her in the morning, she was no assistance at all. The following evening I returned for the last of my three nights, one security guard and no mental health nurse awaited me. Tyson had had an emotional day, he had been on a proper come down. I had spent more time with him that night, he could tell a story better than me, his story of his injuries had transpired to be that of him falling down a verge whilst drunk, no-one else was involved, just him, he was the architect of his own demise.

*

WHAT A YEAR TO QUALIFY

It was the start of May, and it was my final week, just four little shifts to go …

Shift one went over in a flash with no dramas, shift two was not for the faint hearted. Back from more study leave and I had my trusty trainee nurse, Nikki, with me, which was great as we had been allocated eight patients between us. Bed 6 was Alfred, rather rude, obnoxious, and demanding, he had had something to say about everything and anything the day prior and I must admit I was dreading what he had in store for us on this shift. He had started as I had left him the evening previous.

"Can I have this, that, and the other." Generally chastising our every move and making our lives a misery, but Nikki was great with him. He had been in and out his bed three times before 11 a.m., he just didn't seem to settle.

"I'm going to scream," Nikki confessed as she returned from placing him back in bed for the fourth time and it was at this point I had realised after having such a busy morning that actually there could have been more to this than we would have liked to have admitted.

I had finished up the leg dressings of a patient and had made my way to Alfred's bedside, ooh the stench of faeces was overwhelming, I had woken Alfred from a deep sleep, he had appeared weak, very embarrassed of his 'little', actually a rather 'large' accident. I re-assured him there was no need to have been embarrassed and that me and Nikki would clean it up. He had wanted to get out of the bed, but my instinct told me something just wasn't right, so I insisted that he stay in bed until we had finished. My instinct had been right, the faeces was full of dark blood, as though it had been lingering a while. Nikki brought the doctor who wasn't too concerned at that point, he had already arranged for an OGD procedure, short for Oesophago Gastro Duodenoscopy, a camera used for investigations into the stomach and upper part of small intestines. We had cleaned Alfred up just in time for lunch, despite his protests of not wanting any food, Nikki decided to try him with a bit of yogurt.

Moments later …

"Sarah!!" Nikki screamed, the fear in her voice had immediately drawn my attention. Alfred had become unresponsive whilst choking, I reached over and pulled the emergency buzzer for assistance, he had been a very tall man, well over six foot, and although slim in build he weighed a tonne. A doctor had appeared and started lowering the bed.

"For fuck's sake are you for real? He's fucking choking!" I couldn't help myself, it just came out. I insisted that she help us pull him forward whilst I got the suction in his mouth and Bingo! that was all it needed, the airway was clear, and Alfred was suddenly back in the room. The doctors had reviewed him, he had aspirated (the yogurt had basically regurgitated out the stomach and back up), nil by mouth until after he had had is OGD.

No less than thirty minutes later and we were back at Alfred's bedside, I could smell the iron from his blood, Alfred was very weak at this point, he had advised us of another accident.

"Sorry ladies," he said weakly. As I had turned Alfred on his side, his anus facing me, a melon-sized blood clot had slowly dislodged itself from Alfred's back passage. I had ordered Nikki to get a doctor but what she returned with is still questionable. Two Junior Doctors had appeared from behind the curtain, one looked down at the bed which was home to this clot bigger than your standard football, she had looked at the other doctor and rolled her eyes.

"It looks like faeces to us." I picked the clot up with both hands and stretched it in its entirety.

"Are we looking at the same thing?" I had responded, the look on their faces was priceless.

"Put the call out for major haemorrhage," I ordered; they practically fell over one another to get that call out. As I had looked up, Nikki was stood on the opposite side of the bed helping Alfred stay on his side, she looked horrified, I still had this humungous clot in my hands.

"I want to be like you when I qualify," she gasped.

"Thanks, but not my finest hour," was all I could muster in response. The doctor who I had showed the faeces to earlier made a reappearance along with the crash team and they were astounded. *How was he still alive?* The plan was fluids, three unit's frozen plasma, three units of blood and tranexamic acid, this was as serious as it got. The next hour saw us squeezing blood and fluid bags into Alfred until he had stabilised. It was futile, no matter what we were pumping in was coming out just as quick, he was rushed to theatre for an emergency OGD to see if they could stop the internal bleeding.

An hour or so had passed and Alfred was transferred back down, they had been unable to find the cause or location of the bleed. The plan was to continue with plasma and blood as planned and his family would be invited in to see him. After the procedure, he was to remain still and under no circumstance be moved as this had the potential to dislodge and cause more damage. Minimum of two hours we had been advised.

His family had arrived not long after he had returned from his procedure. Nikki advised that he was still bleeding, and it had started to come through the sheets. There was nothing we could have done at this point, Alfred was drifting in and out of consciousness, we packed towels (a lot of towels) between Alfred's legs and placed a clean sheet and blanket over the top.

"Please be enough so it didn't seep through whilst the family are here," I whispered, half to myself and half to Nikki. I had explained the reasons for all the fluids and the bag of blood that was being administered, when a quiet, sheepish voice piped up.

"Am I going to die, Sarah?" It had been Alfred and suddenly all eyes turned to me. I had been in worst situations, believe it or not, in the past eight months and it was a question that was usually asked several times a day when dealing with distressed Covid patients.

"Let's concentrate on the now," had been my usual response or something to that effect, "save your words for Mary and John," (Alfred's wife and son) I had encouraged. I had every notion he was going to die, it was just a matter of when. His family knew this also, they hadn't wanted to believe it, but they knew.

John and Mary left after thirty minutes or so, they were so appreciative of our care.

"You might have the shittiest football team but you're an amazing nurse," John told me as he left, and he was right, Newcastle did have a crap team.

I had called the doctor to review Alfred; it didn't matter what we were putting in it was still coming out twice over. He had agreed the plan needed to be finished, then they would review and make their decision on further interventions. I was really saddened by this decision, the last two hours of the shift saw Nikki and I doing what can only best be described as scooping up buckets full of blood clots, every thirty minutes we checked and cleaned until the night staff took over.

Alfred finished his plan and after the final unit of blood the team had called defeat, he continued to bleed, thankfully sedated, until he passed in the early hours of that morning.

What I would have given to hear Alfred complain, moan, and demand just one more time.

*

Two shifts remained and I was to finish these on the female bay, to top it off I only had three patients on my side as one was a bariatric patient and had left no room for another next to her.

Ethel was her name, she was Scottish, she had dark mousey brown hair with patches of grey running through it. She weighed in at just short of thirty stone, she had been a regular on the unit pre-Covid times and was known for her demands and anger issues. She had bruised and scratched the night staff, grabbing one by the shoulder and sticking her nails in the other's arm. Great! Not what I had needed to finish off my time here.

I had made a rookie error of approaching her first.

"Get me up on this bed!" she demanded and as much as I would have loved to have been able to assist, it was not possible, she had become a four-person job

"I'll be there in a minute, just need to get some assistance," I assured her. She had refused her breakfast and medications until she had been made comfortable, if that's the way it was going to be then she would have to wait until help became available. My other two ladies were elderly, one fully independent and due for discharge that day and the other a dementia sufferer who was pleasantly confused, they had been easy to sort, very compliant with their medications and happy for assistance, despite the running commentary from Ethel on 'what a useless Welsh nurse' I was.

Being Scottish as she was, Ethel had known fine well that I was a Geordie. I hadn't bitten to her sarcastic comments, but this shift would see exactly what a good nurse I was. It had taken four of us to turn, clean, and get her up the bed, not that she had appreciated our efforts, the amount of abuse and use of bad language was unrepeatable. The doctors had requested that her leg dressings be changed, I had duly planned to do it, they were rotten to say the least and the last documented change had been over a week prior. I had enlisted the assistance from the male bay and a Student Nurse was appointed to my rescue. Ethel had been happy to have her leg dressings off, even so much so that mid-way through she decided to pull her cannula out, causing what could have only been described as a minor blood bath.

"No more," she begged. "Let me die." She was acting like it was the end of the world and we'd only removed her leg dressings. Ethel had been making no sense, her legs were doing great, so the decision had been to leave the dressings off. She continued to throw her fists at anyone who attempted to put a cannula back in, and I don't mean the little scrunched up fist of Dot, Ethel's were big boulders of fists intent on causing harm.

The doctors were less than amused at Ethel's actions and attitude, they needed to do a blood test to determine if in fact she was dying or was there more that could be done, she had to this point been in hospital over six months, bounced from ward to ward as very few could tolerate her behaviour. Ethel was calmly scribbling in her book (this was something that she had focussed on a lot, lots of pens and books never to be touched or moved from her table). A young doctor appeared fresh faced with a big smile.

"Do you think she would let me take some blood?" The honest answer was 'No', but who am I to judge?

"Use your charm and ask her," I said instead, so off he went.

"Fuck off ye bastard!" Ethal's booming Scottish accident vertebrated around the ward. It all went quiet until a moment later when the doctor re-appeared.

"She said no." *No shit Sherlock, the whole hospital had heard her!* Obviously, I hadn't said that out loud.

"Better luck next time," was what I said. The poor thing was horrified.

Not one to shirk a challenge (or a drama) I had decided on approaching Ethel immediately after the doctor's departure, I had made it clear to her that her behaviour was intolerable and exhausting. Yep, she told me to 'Fuck off!' too. *At least I wasn't a bastard*, I thought to myself.

Lunch had finally arrived, Ethel happily eating her mac and cheese that had smelt like baby vomit. Halfway through she had decided it was nap time and now lay out cold, snoring like an angry bear and with the stinking food all down her bed and arms. It was little past 1 p.m. and I had felt like I had completed three shifts, never mind not even being halfway through one. I had assistance as we slowly removed the food and cleaned up Ethel. She didn't stir. I wished it would have stayed that way, just for the next six and a half hours.

I discharged one of my little old ladies around 4 p.m., Ethel had still been sleeping, when a lovely tall blonde man in scrubs entered the unit.

"I've come for blood. Bed 21," he commanded. *Great, let's wake the beast*, I thought in my head.

"Over here," a little voice had sounded, it was the young doctor from earlier. *What a brave soul*, I thought, *back for seconds with his big brother*. This was going to be fun. They didn't disappoint, they had woken Ethel from her sleep, who surprisingly was quite polite when woken, she had agreed to the femoral stab, as her wrists were bandaged due to herself removal of cannulas and poor circulation. Now I could have told them that a thirty stone, five-foot, four-inch woman with exceptionally oedematous (swollen – full of fluid) legs was not appropriate for a femoral stab, there was no way they were getting in there, but who am I, a simple nurse. I sat patiently watching with my little old lady who unfortunately was placed opposite Ethel, she had dementia and thought we were watching a film, how sweet she was, a little blessing in disguise. Ethel did not disappoint.

"Ye fucking idiots! Take yer fucking hands off me, this is abuse!" She was screaming hysterically by this point, the doctors had no idea what to do. They had glanced at me at least twice for back up, but I would surface in my own time, which was seconds later, it felt like minutes but was definitely seconds.

"That's enough!" I encouraged Ethel, bringing her hands down from the air.

"Get off me!" she screamed.

"STOP!" I shouted just the once which was enough to startle her into silent compliance. I persisted in holding her hands whilst the doctors (who even I suspected to be idiots at this point), continued to search for the artery. Needless to say, they gave up, responding with a mumbled "She isn't dying, nor is she confused."

As the evening progressed, Ethel had become more confused, she had refused all her medications, her dinner, and was now refusing to drink. I handed over my concerns to the doctors who assured me that they would have the Night Team review.

"Good night, Ethel," I said on my way out.

"Good riddance," she growled in response. I hadn't taken it personally, she was really confused after all, and she was most likely a good, polite person when well.

The following morning, I entered the female unit to see a tall, slim, very well-groomed woman by Ethel's bed and asleep in a chair at the foot of the bed, a tall old man with his flat cap covering half his face. I knew what this had meant, she'd been made end of life throughout the evening, not how I had wanted to spend my last shift, but it was not about me, it was never about me. I had greeted the daughter Sandra as soon as I could.

"How long will this take?" she asked, blunt and to the point. I thought she had meant what was the time it would take me to complete my round but what she had actually been referring to was the length of time it was going to take for her mother to die. I was startled, she was Ethel's daughter, direct and to the point, how wrong was I. It transpired over events of the morning and conversations I had with her family that Ethel was as she had been the day prior throughout her life. 'Never speak ill of the dead', my mam always told me, so I won't. Everyone is different, life experiences sculpt us to who we are, I am a firm believer in that. Ethel had come from a strict upbringing, that had been all she had known, unfortunately she had enforced that on her three children with sadly only one now willing to be at her bedside as a result, as she slowly passed.

Ethel's husband, John, was a character. He has had a tough time of it with Ethel as his wife, but he clearly loved her, insisting she had her moments but was a good person at heart. Despite the daughter's protests, I am sure he was right. I looked at Ethel as she lay peacefully, reminiscing how her last words to me had been 'Good riddance', that just summed her up really.

It was lunchtime and the team had thrown a huge party for me leaving. I was showered with gifts and overwhelmed with sentiments, some had come in on their day off to see me off with their beautiful children in tow. Nursing through Covid together, spending most our lives together over nineteen long hard weeks, had irreversibly changed us all and brought us together, forging a bond which was to be unbreakable.

Fed and watered I returned to Ethel, her husband and daughter had gone home for a few hours ago. She was peacefully sleeping. What a mammoth job it was going to be to do last offices, I shamefully thought. Ethel lasted a further 44 hours before passing with her husband and daughter by her side, I always believed that grief brings people together but throughout my nine months this had been proven to not always be true, more so in Ethel's son's case. He was less than a mile from the hospital and never even called or visited to say his last goodbyes.

CHAPTER 16

FINAL THOUGHTS

I had completed my final shift, the following morning I had to start the mammoth task of packing for the move back to Newcastle in less than 72 hours.

I took the opportunity to go through my bags of gifts from the team, their words of endearment and encouragement in my cards, gifts, some had been personalised just for me. I had been completely overwhelmed. What a journey we had all been on. I had started in London as a newly qualified nurse, I had completed my preceptorship and was no longer under the premise of newly qualified, I had experienced more than the average nurse would experience in their lifetime, the nurse I was destined to be. I had watched so many people struggle and die at the hand of Covid. I had held so many hands, wishing them to just breathe. I had pushed myself to my limits. I had given more when more was not possible. I had been supported by the most caring colleagues and surrounded by the unconditional love of my family; I was the only winner in my eyes.

Nursing through a pandemic as a newly qualified nurse was tough but if I had the same opportunity and my time again, I would not change a thing. Decisions were made, some questionable at times, but these times were unprecedented. We did what we thought was best for our patients and I wouldn't want it any other way. I was not alone in my journey, unique as my perspective may seem. Across the world nurses, doctors, and healthcare's were and are still going through exactly what I had experienced. They are all the true heroes of the pandemic.

ABOUT THE AUTHOR

Before embarking on my career as a nurse, I had always worked in a corporate environment (people and project management). After returning from three years in Australia in 2014 with the family, I made the decision to return to education and train as a nurse, my husband commuted to London during this time to support me in my studies.

In my final year of training, my son was offered a scholarship to the NFL American football academy in Tottenham, which saw him and my husband relocating to London permanently. As I was in my final year of study I was unable to join them so myself and my daughter (who took a year out of starting University) stayed in Newcastle for that final year, splitting our family in two.

WHAT A YEAR TO QUALIFY

On completion of my degree in August 2020, and becoming a qualified nurse, myself and my daughter moved to London to be with the boys, and here is where the story for my book began.

Needless to say, I was overwhelmed by relocating amidst a pandemic to the Nation's capital and my experiences there were not for the faint hearted. Not only was I a newly qualified nurse, I was also far from family and colleagues who I had trained with.

The book was initially a project for myself on my experiences and the impact that it had on myself, my family, my colleagues, but most importantly the patients I had cared for. After receiving feedback from independent readers and family I agreed to seek publication.

The aim of the book is to give readers an insight into the struggles of the pandemic for frontline staff and to share the highs and lows of the pandemic first-hand, it's about inspiration and the unbreakable bonds between patients, families, and colleagues.

These times were unprecedented, politics can often get in the way of looking at the reality of what we are/have lived through and hopefully this book will inspire future nurses and give a greater understanding of how every contact we have, no matter how minor, has the potential to change lives. I am still a practising nurse within the Newcastle upon Tyne Hospital Trust and hope I am continuing to inspire.

Printed in Great Britain
by Amazon